The Diary of Losing Dad

The Diary of
Losing Dad

EMILY BEVAN

unbound

First published in 2022

Unbound
Level 1, Devonshire House, One Mayfair Place, London W1J 8AJ
www.unbound.com

Text design by PDQ Digital Media Solutions Ltd.

A CIP record for this book is available from the British Library

ISBN 978-1-80018-080-2 (hardback)
ISBN 978-1-80018-081-9 (ebook)

Printed in Great Britain by CPI Group (UK)

1 3 5 7 9 8 6 4 2

This book is for my family.
And for our little sunbeam, Romy.

With thanks to the book's patron,
Shiplake College.

'Grief is the small print of love'
Erica Buist, *This Party's Dead*

Contents

Contents

Prologue

It feels rather grand to be writing a prologue. I could have opted for a simple introduction, but if you only get the chance to publish one book, why not get the most out of the experience?

At the centre of this piece is my father, Nick Bevan, who was blessed with having had a very full and fascinating life. He was deeply modest, but with a bit of coaxing would regale you with wonderful stories, such as the time he met Muhammad Ali in the jungle, was mistaken for a cowboy in America by a bunch of Japanese tourists, and how, in 1962, he travelled across Europe in a Rolls-Royce to visit his friend Harald, the Crown Prince of Norway. I never tired of hearing these anecdotes.

If you had met my dad, you would probably have recognised that he was a man with a big personality. A gentle soul who bounded around, Tigger-like with energy, full of positivity and a wonderful sense of humour. He seized life, and life seemed to seize him back. He had many interests and passions and was never bored.

In 1988, when I was just six years old, we arrived at a spectacularly located independent boys' school, where my father was taking up the 'Top Job', as it's described in educational circles. I was bursting with pride at his new appointment, something that was clearly demonstrated on my first day at the local primary school, when I proudly announced to everyone who would listen, 'My name is Emily Bevan and MY FATHER IS THE HEADMASTER OF SHIPLAKE COLLEGE.' Dad was my hero, someone who I felt epitomised all that was good, fair and kind. He was exactly six foot tall, but seemed far taller in my estimation, and was always fit, active and full of life. As a small child, I clung to his sturdy legs, peering out behind them at the big wide world beyond.

I loved walking the short two minutes from home (through the school orchard) to visit him in his study at Shiplake. A room that overlooked the River Thames, it was lined with leather-bound books, and smelled of photocopying and Alta Rica coffee. I would tap on the window, often disturbing him as he spoke into his Dictaphone VE-RY CLEAR-LY AND CARE-FUL-LY. The kitchen in his office was always my first port of call, reliably stocked as it was with gourmet chocolate biscuits, specially bought in to charm any prospective families that might come by. I observed him closely at his work, picking up strange habits for a child, including answering our home phone with, 'Emily Bevan speaking, how can I help you?' and beginning letters to friends with, 'Dear Sir/Madam. I am writing to inform you that I am very well.'

As I'm sure other offspring of teachers will understand it was a bit strange, having a father who was a headmaster, because for me he was just 'Dad'; the accident-prone man who loved Marmite and peanut butter sandwiches, John Grisham thrillers, and sent us purposefully misspelt birthday cards from the dog.

None of my friends had the humbling experience of their dad being invited as a special guest to their end-of-school ball, where he stood at the side of the room, winking furiously and giving them a thumbs up. Indeed, he was on the panel for

choosing the best dancer and was completely impartial and
neutral and decided that it should be awarded to me. Nor were
they made to drive forty-five minutes down the M40 when
they wanted to 'pop out to the cinema', lest their father be
seen eating popcorn, wearing Levi's and ordering a deep-pan
pepperoni pizza. I also remember meeting one of Dad's 'new
friends' at a Shiplake school concert: a very nice lady with a
comfortable shoulder, which I promptly fell asleep on. I doubt
many other people had this first experience of meeting their
future headmistress.

At university, Dad still managed to cast an influence. In my
second year, I rented a house with five friends. The landlord
was a graduating third-year student who, as Dad would say,
turned out to be a 'bit of a crook'. When we arrived at the house
in September, the place looked like it had just played host
to a massive house party: the oven caked in grease, building
materials falling out of cupboards, the garden full of junk, and
seedy red light bulbs in the sockets. When Dad got wind of this,
I don't think our poor new landlord knew what had hit him.
I imagine he was made to feel as though he had been caught
smoking behind the bus stop and sentenced to a lifetime in
detention. A threat was made that if things weren't sorted by
the following evening, Dad was going to track him down and
kill him. Sorry, no, that's Liam Neeson. But you get the idea.
Minutes after Dad's terrifying phone call, grovelling apologies
were made to each of us, refunds were offered, the house was
miraculously cleaned and whipped into shape.

That protectiveness never went away. Dad was always
interested in everything that I was doing and sent me
countless emails offering advice. Once such email went along
the lines of 'NONE of my business, TEAR IT UP, tell me

I'm talking RUBBISH, but hope this might help a bit,' as I was considering moving out of London. And then attached was a Word document broken down into 'pluses', 'minuses', 'ACTION POINTS' and finished off with '2 important fatherly points' for good measure. Followed by 'DO come back to me and tell me I'm talking NONSENSE'. His emails – regardless of the content – were always full of CAPITALS to emphasise his point better. I miss seeing his name pop up in my inbox.

The memories and stories that follow are reconstructed from diaries I kept during the painful and intense months of late 2013 and early 2014, during which Dad became increasingly unwell. At the time, words and feelings were spilling out of me, often quite chaotically, onto the page. My journals became my 'friendly pages' – somewhere to offload, to record precious details and try to create beauty and meaning where things were painful and out of control.

Dad died on 12 January 2014 at the John Radcliffe Hospital in Oxford. I stopped writing my journal a week or so later. I hadn't been back to the John Radcliffe until this year, in May 2020, when, in a strangely comforting twist of fate, I returned there to bring a new life into the world: my daughter Romy. Thus the story comes full circle.

Due to coronavirus, I am back at my family home, and find myself editing this book sitting at Dad's desk, surrounded by his books, rowing memorabilia, photographs and even a few old hats.

Dad loved children, particularly his four grandchildren: Penny and Sophia, from my eldest brother Ed and his wife Debs; and Maia and Toby, from my sister Kate and her husband Charlie. I think he would be pleased that his study has yet again become a miniature playground, strewn with a rainforest playmat and countless colourful toys. A plastic parrot is currently blasting out a mechanical rendition of 'Skip to My Lou, My Darling'. I never imagined my first attempts at writing a book would be accompanied by such a soundtrack. I guess life goes on; the parrot certainly blasts on. Painful memories are slowly etched into by newer, brighter ones.

Anyway, I'll stop here. As my mum has kindly just pointed out, 'You don't want to bore everyone before you've even started.' Cheers, Mum.

JULY 2012

Dad's Evil Kidney
17 July 2012

When my dad is first diagnosed with renal cancer, I am twenty-nine years old, and I deal with this life-changing news with humour and bad poetry.

I give him a card on 17 July 2012, with the caption 'Devastating Man' on the front. Inside I have written a poem entitled 'Ode to Dad's EVIL kidney'. The bamboo in the third line refers to an incident in which he almost poked his eye out in the garden...

> Now, Dad, it's time that down we sat
> and had ourselves a little chat.
> First bamboo, and then the heart –
> your health has given us a start.
> But now a kidney? Er, no no;
> I'm sorry, but it's got to go.
> Not both, but just the 'evil twin';
> the ugly one – we'll call him Jim.
> He's draining you of energy
> and giving nothing back, you see.
> You just don't need that in your life
> (you get enough gyp from your wife).
> So farewell, Jim, the end is nigh,
> go pack your bags and say goodbye.

> Your number's up, you little cad,
> Now keep your fingers off my dad.

After his diagnosis, we lament the fact that we had not picked up on something sooner. He had lost weight, certainly, but he had been steadily shedding pounds since his heart attack in 2010, after which he'd radically reduced his intake of brie. Fatigue is not a word that you would have formerly associated with Nicholas Vaughan Bevan, a man who had maintained an irritatingly high level of fitness his whole life and whose energy and enthusiasm seemed almost boundless. The crucial alarm bell rang when Dad casually revealed that he'd had to sit down during a morning walk with our much-loved Labrador, Boris. Mum (a retired nurse) immediately dispatched him off to the doctor's surgery and a short time later, a scan revealed a croissant-shaped mass in his right kidney. (This seems particularly cruel given that he was always partial to them.) After a successful operation to remove the cancerous kidney, the surgeon reassured us that there was no evidence that the cancer had spread and was confident Dad was 'unlikely to face any further problems'.

A few notes on Dad and Boris the Labrador

1. Dad sometimes describes Boris as his 'best friend'.
2. When I suggest that Dad should wear headphones and listen to the radio on his twice-daily dog walks, Dad says: 'Bit antisocial for Boris.'
3. When I ask Dad (a modest amateur artist) why he doesn't ever draw Boris – only landscapes and the occasional still life – Dad replies: 'I can't draw people.'

JUNE 2013

Mum's Birthday
5 June 2013

Dad and I have been plotting to take Mum to see *Matilda the Musical* but Dad is bedridden with sciatica. I receive a hurriedly written email from him, once again utilising his 'capital letters for added emphasis' technique, which makes it sound like he's shouting:

> Em
> In haste... I am a bit crook as you know and might not even make it to London. BUT SHE WILL LOVE DOING THE WHOLE THING WITH YOU IF THAT'S THE CASE AND SHE WILL HAVE MY CREDIT CARD WITH HER!
> Sorry to be in a rush but I get uncomfortable sitting at my desk for too long...
> TONS of love
> dad

I book a table for me and Mum at the Hawksmoor restaurant opposite the theatre. I am overdressed for a Tuesday lunchtime but clearly want to project an air of grown-up-actress-living-in-London sophistication and wave my hand casually over the menu, as if nothing is off limits. (I gulp slightly when I see the bill.)

*

As it's her birthday, we order a couple of glasses of champagne. She takes a few tentative sips, before carefully removing her glasses and placing them thoughtfully on the table. She smiles heavily, clears her throat and then calmly explains that Dad's renal cancer has returned.

She tells me that Dad's latest scan has revealed a number of small lesions, or 'shadows', in his chest cavity that need further investigation. We order another drink, and then are presented with two plates of extravagantly priced steak that neither of us wants to eat.

Shortly after we cross over to the Cambridge Theatre to watch *Matilda*. We hold hands and sob all the way through.

JULY 2013

A few facts about renal cancer
1. It can remain dormant for years.
2. It is unpredictable.
3. The new drugs (a form of chemotherapy) that have just become available are thought to be very effective.
4. People who are much worse affected than Dad are doing well seven years on.

After careful consideration and research, Dad agrees with his oncologist that he will start taking the drugs in October, when his much-anticipated summer holidays are over. In the meantime, it is suggested that he and Mum join a support group with other renal cancer sufferers, to get a better idea of the treatment ahead.

Really Good News

On 2 July 2013, Dad sends an email to my brother Oli and me (his two single, youngest children of four) saying that his first experience of the cancer support group was good. Everyone was very positive and it seems the surgeon and specialist are the very best. He says that the really good news is that he's booked a holiday to Tuscany (getting car and flights on Avios points), and:

> IF EITHER OF YOU WANTED TO JOIN US for any or all of the time you would be VERY welcome indeed but be warned flights need booking ASAP and aren't CHEAP!

This is shortly followed up with an email listing all of the available flights, categorised as 'cheap', 'not cheap' and 'very cheap'. He is always making plans. I reply with the following message:

> Hi Dad,
> I'm so sorry for being slow to reply to your email. I was waiting for a quiet moment. I'm so glad the support group was good and that you came away encouraged and feeling reassured. It's clearly doing exactly what it says on the tin. You have been so brave about this recent news. It really is so unfair how life has dealt you such a dodgy hand, but your energy, determination and positivity are incredible – your special superpower. We are all 100 per cent here for you in every way – as are your army of fans. The strangely nice thing about all this bloody illness is that you must feel a lot of love coming your way from many different areas of your life. Judging by the following you have in the Balliol Women's Boat Club, I can see you will be a hit with the nurses

if and when you come into contact with them. I'm extremely proud of you – and love you loads – and will do everything I can to help. Much love xxx

Rereading the email above now, I think how tidy and neat I made his illness sound. Knowing the journey we have been on, it feels a little shallow – like a motivational speech to a colleague. A jumble of jargon: 'one hundred per cent', 'incredible', 'special', 'love', 'pride', 'brave'. I meant it all, of course, but I tied the situation up with a ribbon that made me feel better. It didn't come easily to talk, or even write, about what was going on. I should have replied saying:

Dad,
This is a complete pile of crap. You are the healthiest man I have ever met. You've had a heart attack, cancer, sciatica, and now the bitch is back. I'm so sorry. Please don't feel you have to be positive about it for our sake. If you want to have a moan, or a cry, it would be totally normal to do so. Or go into a field and scream. I'm sure Boris won't mind. I'm so sorry. You are the greatest human. You don't deserve this. I'm angry with the universe and I love you so much, you have no idea. Xxxx

AUGUST 2013

The Italian Holiday
11 August 2013

My birthday. I have been flown up to the Edinburgh Festival to attend a screening of *In the Flesh*,* followed by a Q & A with the writer, Dominic Mitchell.

We meet a range of fans, and are both touched to experience, first-hand, just how much the show means to people. It is a bizarre feeling when someone says to me that they have never met a famous person before. Strange to be seen in that way. There was a very nervous teenager who was trembling when we posed for a photo together. She said that Amy was her favourite character because she goes through tough times but stays positive and good-humoured. When she walked away with her mum – both huddled over her phone, looking at the photos they'd taken – I practically burst into tears.

I'm only needed for a few hours, so afterwards spend the afternoon and evening hopping between friends' shows. I wheel out of a bar at 2 a.m., suitcase in hand, and head to Edinburgh Airport to fly to Rome (my logic is: stay out late, get 'very cheap' early flight = save money on hotel). While successful

* A BAFTA-winning BBC 3 zombie show in which I played one of the leads.

with this, less successful is my ability to get myself from
Rome to the small Tuscan town of Chiusi, where I'm meeting
Mum and Dad. At Stazione Termini I stare hopelessly at the
illuminated orange announcement boards and try to call my
parents without success.

Miraculously, I find my way onto the correct train and, to my
enormous relief, my parents are there to greet me at Chiusi
station. Dad is first to tumble out of their rented Cinquecento,
panama hat first, a vision of pressed pastel linen and smelling
of sun cream and Chanel. I am enveloped in warmth, security,
familiarity. They are effervescent and freckled with sun. So
many happy memories of my parents crystallise around these
larger-than-life meetings and goodbyes. The relief of seeing
them is palpable and I slip effortlessly into their company. To
celebrate my birthday we open a bottle of fizz (as is Bevan
tradition), and I'm presented with an envelope, which reads
'Signora Emily Bevan. In Fontepico'. Inside the card is the
inscription 'Happy Birthday to a Bella Figlia', handwritten by
Dad in his fountain pen.

Observations of being on holiday with parents
1. Dad describes suntan as 'sunburn'.
2. You come away with cleaner clothes than when you arrived.
3. Glasses are worn in the pool.
4. Swimming costumes are referred to as 'bathers'.
5. They sit in the shade.
6. They drink at lunchtime.
7. They have to get up, after sitting down for breakfast, to get their pill.
8. They have a cup of tea and a biscotti at precisely 4.30 p.m.
9. They look for their compression socks.

10. Dad escorts me back to my room every night to make sure I get there OK. It's a metre from theirs.

Tomato Salads Heaped with Parmesan
19 August 2013

When it comes to holidays, I think there are two kinds of people. Those who hunger for new experiences year after year and those who want to revisit and rediscover the same pleasures. Mum and Dad are the latter. They love this corner of Tuscany and are no longer prepared to gamble with their precious summer holiday. The cottage is tucked away under a thick canopy of vines in the corner of a large Tuscan estate, where the only other people you will sometimes encounter are the glamorous *señora* who occasionally drifts across the perfectly manicured lawn in a kaftan with a bottle of Montepulciano, or the gardener, Luciano, whom Dad always greets with an enormous *'Buon-gioouuuuurnnioo, Luciaaaannoo! Ciao ciao,'* patting him on the back furiously and shaking his hand until his very few words of Italian rapidly run out.

Mum reads and sunbathes, making delicious lunches of tomato salad heaped with Parmesan, prosciutto, basil and olive oil. Dad spends his days reading, wrestling with the BBQ and painting watercolours of the Tuscan landscapes. He helps me with an audition tape for a particularly laddish script, enthusiastically reading in the other lines, including one about 'defiling a bridesmaid'. He doesn't bat an eye. When I send off the tapes to my agent, Dad asks me to mention that he is available too. He is only sort-of joking. Afterwards, I take my first ever 'selfie' of us.

Dad's illness is our silent companion, tiptoeing softly into the quiet moments. Ever-present, lingering in the shadows of our conversations. I have a strange feeling, a tug of something in my stomach, on the last morning of the holiday as Dad and I sit together, toes in the water, contemplating our final swim: our 'BBB' (Bathe Before Breakfast), as his family would traditionally call it.

I watch Dad as he sits for a long while on the steps at the side of the pool, studying the ripples that undulate around his feet, enjoying the sensation of moving his hands through the cool water, like a sculler, taking gentle strokes. He is half smiling, half contemplative. Thoughtful. We don't talk. We just sit together, on the edge of something bigger than us. I have a very strong need to take as many pictures of him as I can.

SEPTEMBER 2013

Longest Runner Bean
1 September 2013

Less than a month later, I'm boarding a flight to Berlin when I receive a very cheerful email from Dad. He describes how he and Mum have got on in the hotly anticipated village Flower and Produce Show – an event my brother Oli refers to as 'The Vegetable Olympics'. (You would never guess from Dad's email that he's a highly competitive sportsman with a still unquenchable thirst for silverware.)

From: Nick Bevan
To: Oliver, Emily, Kate, Ed
Subject: The Flower Show... not all results known
Date: 01/09/2013

Dear All
Following an intensely competitive judging marathon provisional results show that Team Bevan have won 2 golds, 2 silvers, a 'highly commended' and almost certainly more to come. Silvers went to Mrs B in the scones and longest runner bean, the latter being lost by a mere millimetre or two. Golds were secured in the cooking apples and limerick. Results are not yet known in many of the flower-arranging and vegetable categories but it will be a travesty if the single rose doesn't medal,

not to mention the 5 blooms or the wild flowers which were both also well up to the mark. But many thanks for your help with the limerick, which caused a few tongues to wag! We'll let you know when we hear of further successes! Good luck to all starting school this week.
We hope the travellers have reached home safely.
And MANY thanks for 2 lovely evenings on Wednesday and Thursday; great fun. Lots of love Dad etc.

Somehow Dad's morning motivational talks to the veg patch had been successful, and he had managed to instil self-belief in our competing legumes. I read the email quickly and reply casually, saying that I'm off to make a short film in Berlin and that I'm devastated Mum wasn't the 'Queen of the Beans'. I'm distracted and bubbling over with excitement at heading to my favourite city. And this time for work, not play.

A few notes on Berlin and me

1. On my first ever night out in Berlin I fell in love three times.
2. On my second night out I calmed down and fell in love only once.
3. I discovered techno there. (About ten years after everybody else.)
4. I find the place effortlessly cool and endlessly stimulating.
5. I find the people effortlessly cool and endlessly stimulating.
6. I discovered *Eier im Glas* there. Eggs in a glass. Two boiled eggs in a glass with cress chopped on top and salt and pepper.
7. Example night out in Berlin: an art gallery to a museum to an opera in an old swimming pool* to a book launch to a bar to a restaurant to a bar* to a club to a club.*
8. In the art galleries, I stare more at the Berliners than at the art itself. The tall, handsome, bearded men. The bobbed

women with coats elegantly perched on their shoulders, whose red-lipsticked mouths twist in scrutiny as they take in an exhibit. They all look like they could be the artist. Or the artist's lover.

9. Even the taxis in Berlin are cooler than London cabs. SORRY. They have blacked-out windows, low black-leather seats, and overall just give you a 'David Hasselhoff in *Knight Rider*' sort of feeling as you sweep down the wide streets, past the vast imposing architecture and the smoky hidden bars.

10. There is a promise of something.

*Fell in love

A New Normal

2 September 2013

I am in Berlin to make a short film with my very good friend Lea, a writer, director and producer. We have wanted to collaborate together on something for a long time. She has assembled a crew and has rented an Airbnb flat in a large Soviet block, which has been dressed up as our location. We spend the first day chatting the story through over bagels and shopping for a costume. That night we go out for something that is known in the German film world as 'warm-up drinks' and I meet the majority of the crew. The next day is our first day of filming. In a break between rehearsals and the start of the shoot, I go back to Lea's flat to get changed into my costume. I connect to wi-fi and am flooded with messages.

Call. Call home, Em. Call us when you can. Facebook. Email. Text. WhatsApp.

Clearly something is very wrong. I try to call my brother Oli's mobile but can't get through. I text him saying, 'Tell me Mum and Dad are OK?' He replies saying that he will call me when he gets home.

I wait. Sitting glued to the spot, phone resting in my hand. When the phone rings, I immediately answer and there is a muffled sound of the phone being passed, and then Mum speaks. She tells me that Dad has had a stroke. It had happened as they were getting ready to go out. His arm had felt weak, she had rushed him to the doctor's surgery but by the time they got there he was paralysed down his left-hand side. She says that she is feeling calmer now, but that it was a huge shock. Her voice starts to crack and Oli takes the phone.

Now I learn how serious this is. Oli calmly explains that 'we need to find a new normal'. A *new normal*. I carefully collect the information that I'm being given, but I feel utterly numb. The words sit on my skin. As the youngest child of four, I am accustomed to having bad news softened for me, mashed up with a fork to make it more palatable, but this is too big to throw a veil over. So big, in fact, that I can't really fathom it. I am dry-eyed and eerily calm; in shock, I suppose. It's one of those huge life moments where you might hope that the clouds would part in your mind, and you'd have an almost heroic sense of clarity and understanding, knowing precisely what to say and what to do. In stark contrast, I am completely lost. There's a film crew a few miles away patiently waiting for me to arrive, and back home in the UK my dad is very seriously ill – perhaps even dying. I don't know what to do. I stare straight ahead. 'Tell me what to do.' Mercifully my brother takes control and instructs me to stay in Berlin and make the film. He says that it's 'awful' back at home, that it would be better for me to return

in a few days when things have calmed down. He says that they
will really look forward to seeing me. That he will book me
a flight.

A subplot

By the time I get over to the film set, everybody in the crew
knows. I smile optimistically, upbeat, wanting to carry on
as normal. People look at me with concern and I brush off
any fuss saying, 'I'm fine, really.' They tell me that I'm in
shock. My friend Lea gives me the tightest hug, her eyes
full, brimming with understanding. I'm very aware of how I
should be feeling. What the appropriate reaction to this news
should be. But something about the distance from home,
the timing, the situation, means it just isn't sinking in. Try
as I might, I cannot push 'Dad' and 'stroke' into the same
sentence.

The crew speak in German, so I'm ignorant of what's going
on around me most of the time. I am in my own little world.
Instead of saying 'action' when the cameras are rolling, like we
do in the UK, there is a polite call of *'Und bitte!'* Instead of 'cut'
the Germans say, *'Und danke'.* The film has no dialogue, but
gently unravels from moment to moment. We're shooting at
night, so there's a dreamy quality to the experience. I feel like
I'm floating; not really rooted in reality but in a strange, half-
fictional hinterland, surrounded by new, kind faces.

When I meet Leo, the director of photography, I smile hello and
ask, 'How are you?' He considers me for a long moment and
says, 'Better than you, I think.' He likes my t-shirt, decorated
with an animal-print cross. Saintly. Devilish. I like how he
refers to objects as 'him'. Our hands find each other in the dark
stairwell. He places a gentle hand on the bottom of my back,

guiding me into the scene I'm playing. I collect new words that float around the room, finding in them mystery and absolutely no meaning. And totally unconsciously, he becomes the life raft to which I cling.

At 3 a.m. the following night we are pushing his broken-down car along an empty street to revive it. We kiss in a doorway, and drink whiskey in a tiny, smoky, neon-lit bar until dawn. I am 623 miles from home. He says, 'Maybe this is the start of our story.'

On the last night, after we wrap filming, we head out into the early hours. We speed across the city in Leo's car, with the windows down, blasting out 'Bad Kingdom' by Moderat. I feel intensely alive, selfishly clinging to these last few hours of ignorant freedom. Our destination is Berghain, Berlin's most famous and intimidating techno club. I want the night to go on and on.

I leave Berghain at 5 a.m. I shower and dress hurriedly, wear sunglasses as I walk through customs and immediately fall asleep on the plane. I nearly miss a connection. I need to pee so badly when I wake up that I have to battle the tide of passengers trying to get off the plane. I am in a dream. I am thinking about Leo. A power supply pulled out and another one plugged in. He tells me to make my reunion 'beautiful'. My heart still carries the bass of Berlin. A thrumming in my ears.

Oli meets me in the car park beneath the airport and we sit soberly together in Dad's car, his hands gripping the steering wheel. He talks me through the situation at home and tells me what to expect. He says that Dad is crying a lot; that he's different, but still there. Again he talks about this 'new normal', which I am yet to discover, let alone comprehend. Oli is going into London for a couple of nights to have a much-needed break, so he gives me the car keys and some Valium tablets from Mum, in case I need them. (Human Valium, rather than our dog's Valium, which Oli had found Mum chopping up in the kitchen at 6 a.m. the day after Dad's stroke. She was determined that he wouldn't see her cry.)

I should not be driving. I get out of the maze underneath Heathrow Airport and onto the motorway that is dazzling with headlights. I blink into the early evening traffic – M4, M40 – with no idea what to expect at the other end.

First Sight
7 September 2013

I walk through the vast concrete maze of wings and signs at the John Radcliffe, eventually making it into a lift. It pings. Everything is in slow motion. I glide through each door (the Valium is kicking in). Time, seconds lengthen. Stretch. Drawn out by anticipation that is both desperate to see him and fearful of what or who I will find. I am completely lost. A kind man steers me to the right place. I sterilise my hands and pass a sea of curious eyes. And then at the end of the ward...

You
Lopsided
But unmistakable.
Oh, Dad.

You cry floods. I have never seen you truly cry before. And I had not prepared myself for this.

You are so happy to see me and squeeze my hand in the tightest grip. I kiss and stroke your head. Touch the cool skin of your left arm, which lies lifeless on a little pillow. A layer has been taken off and I can see so much in your eyes. You are achingly vulnerable. Achingly loveable.

For an Oxford man, it strikes me, for the first time, that your eyes are the wrong shade of blue. Pools of pale grey stare enquiringly at me. I ask what you're looking at, and you say, 'I'm looking at my beautiful daughter.' A kindly nurse approaches and asks, 'Is this your grandpa?'

Do Not Bend
I'd like to wrap you up in bubble-wrap
with all my dearest things.
Put you in a square box.
Muffled. Safe.
Carefully fold the box around your form and sellotape
the edges.
Snug.
I'd look after you.

(I'd cut a hole so you could breathe.)

Uprooted
Four children grew under a shady tree
and the tree was you
and the youngest of the children was me.
When lightning struck, the tree fell.
They heard the terrible sound and, frightened, hid indoors,
until it was quiet.
At the bottom of the garden, the tree lay,
its great stature becoming shadow.

At this height, they could look at it more closely.
They noticed things they had never seen before.
The tree needed them.
It hurt when they sat on it.
'Ouch,' said the tree.
Can we stand you up again?

Dad has an ebullience and positivity that is infectious. When I was nervous about school exams, he'd take the sting out of them by telling me to 'Enjoy them, Em!' Everything in life was seen as a challenge or an opportunity for growth. Even mundane daily tasks like ironing and washing-up would be attacked with dynamism and competitive spirit – and there was always the offer of a 'prize'. Usually a sloppy kiss. His pep and gusto occasionally got him into trouble, and he was alarmingly accident-prone, particularly in the garden, where he once very nearly poked his eye out on a bamboo cane and regularly injured his hands. He was also prone to thumping his head on the low door frames of our family home, Mill Cottage, always followed by a booming 'RUGGER!', 'BOLLARDS! or 'SHIVERS!' Years spent in the education system had made him a master of sanitised swearing.

Despite the constant worry and exhaustion, we are determined to pull together as a family and remain positive, à la NVB. Among all the anxiety and worry there are precious moments of lightness. We cry and laugh so much that we decide that we need to find a new word for crying and laughing at the same time... craughing?

A conversation between Dad, Oli and me:

Dad This has been...

*Oli and I look at each other and gulp, steeling ourselves for a big
emotional revelation.*
Oli (gently) What, Dad?
Dad This has been...
Oli Go on, Dad. You can say it.
Dad No – this is BING (pointing at a nurse).

Dad knows Bing's name, and indeed the names of everyone
who works on the ward and is careful to introduce us to them
individually. He is full of gratitude for their care, and softly and
sibilantly says, 'These people are brilliant.' The porter, Victor
('a very good man'), is gentle in manner and voice. He wheels
along to deliver Dad's supper at about 5 p.m. and Dad greets
him warmly, despite his unappetising cargo. His nurse, Nisha,
is energetic and caring but also quite strict, wanting to push
her patients on the stroke ward as far as possible, aware of the
enormous journey that lies ahead of them. It is too enormous a
concept to comprehend: bringing half of your body back to life.
She grills me on my dancing and singing ability and then tells
me, quite seriously, that with my pale skin and dark hair, I must
go and conquer Bollywood.

Visiting Time
8 September 2013

When I arrive at visiting time, Dad is just finishing a pencil
drawing of Andrew, the patient in the bed opposite – perhaps
the only portrait he's ever drawn. I notice that Dad has signed
his masterpiece at the bottom. He is bubbling over with
empathy for his fellow stroke-sufferer and wants me to take the
picture over to Andrew, who is leaving that day, and give it to
him as a parting gift. Dad weeps uncontrollably when he places

the picture in my hands, nodding enthusiastically as I walk across the room to his vacant (and I think half-sedated) ward-fellow. Andrew takes it, looking slightly confused, but I reassure Dad afterwards that it was a very special moment. *I wonder if Andrew still has it. If it meant anything to him.*

Another of his ward-fellows, Ralph, is a beaming man in his eighties or perhaps even nineties. Upsettingly, Ralph sleeps through the entirety of his granddaughter's visit, and wakes up distressed, repeatedly asking for 'my Julia'. It is utterly heart-breaking to behold. He looks at me with glittering eyes and says, 'You are a gorgeous girl.' I blush and thank him, and he says, 'I speak only the truth.' After a pause he then adds, 'What deck are we on?'

The tables have turned, and the headmaster now has homework. He has daily sessions with an occupational therapist and also a speech therapist. Regaining his balance and learning how to swallow properly again are all important first steps. He has a sheet of tongue-twisters that he has to practise daily. His voice is much smaller, whispery, less sure inside its body. As an actor, I have a few tongue-twisters up my sleeve, and suggest we have a go at 'I'm not a pheasant plucker, I'm the pheasant-plucker's son, and I'll be plucking pheasants till the pheasant plucker comes', which he fails to see the humour in and instead attempts with such focus that it looks like his eyeballs might roll together, like marbles, and meet in the middle. He is immediately all-embracing of any suggestion, seizing on it, entirely open, entirely vulnerable and determined to get better.

The sentence 'give the dog a biscuit' causes his eyes to well up. Boris.

*

Each burst of tears starts with a pained frown, which moves down to a wrinkle of the nose (as if he might sneeze), to a wobble of the chin, which moves through the lower lip until it sticks right out, like it could catch tears from heaven, which are surely falling in pity at this sight. It is a shuddering, devastating cry that feels out of his control.

Changing the subject and distracting him is a technique that we quickly learn to master, but it can feel like trying to keep a car from swerving off the road. When we announce that my brother Ed is coming to visit from Dubai, Dad's eyes fill with wonder and emotion; the nose starts the ill-fated wrinkle. His small, amazed voice: 'To see me?' We nod. 'On a *plane*?' It's agonising and adorable and heartbreaking and hilarious. There are sudden outbursts of frustration too: 'It's *awful* when you're not here. I *hate* it.'

Interspersed with the emotional highs and lows are moments of practicality and clarity. He wants pyjamas with a fly (to help preserve his dignity when he needs a pee), and he wants me to make sure that Mum is OK. That Boris has been walked and made a fuss of.

His glasses, or 'specs', as he calls them, always sit wrongly. One of the arm ends now sits inside his left ear, rather than on top of it. He can't feel it or is too tired to care. It is unbelievably loveable in its wonkiness.

Despite the agony of the situation, Dad's sense of humour remains intact. On one of the terribly anxious first days in hospital, Dad manages to break the tense atmosphere with his comment about the hospital shepherd's pie. After taking a tentative mouthful he says, 'My compliments to the chef. Absolutely revolting.' We are amused, yet not surprised to discover that the hospital food is provided by a construction company, seemingly running a mere sideline in catering. Perhaps that night's meal had been prepared in a cement mixer.

Her

There's a hole in the house.
The furniture has moved.
This little home
where a man's voice filled every room.

Slowly stretching out, she's taking up the space.
Her faltering voice, given breath.
People to call.
Thank you all.

Always doing, doing, done, occupied completely
but completely incomplete without
him.

'He needs me.'
He does.
Everything is *her* now.
He sits, picturing her face
until she enters the room.

There are some memorable visits from family. Dad's elder brother Tim, a retired brigadier, comes to visit, bringing enormous cheer and light relief to the ward. He reads Dad dirty limericks from a book that we've been given and they giggle like schoolboys. His sense of humour post-stroke is definitely more mischievous. Tim is told off for trying to smuggle Dad a 'snorker' (sausage) from the catering trolley. Food is strictly pureed for now. As Tim leaves, he tells the nurses to 'look after my little brother' and says to me conspiratorially, 'Let me know when he's fit for sausages and I'll smuggle some in.'

Dad's younger brother Richard comes over especially from Seattle, and is wonderful and gentle with him. He is clearly shocked by Dad's state, and through his eyes I am reminded of how changed he is. When tired, Dad is distracted, negative, visibly strained. It is utterly unlike him.

When it's time for Rich to leave the hospital, I walk him to the lift and he gives me a big hug and says that it's going to be OK, but I think neither of us are sure if it will. We hold hands and share something profound and unspoken, both desperately worried. Richard has brought us a copy of his recently completed family memoir, and it brings Dad huge pleasure when we read out passages from it. He remembers the past with relish, soaking up the memories, comforted by happy tales of his childhood. He says 'yes' so quickly with recognition at a forgotten detail, like a little child.

Aunt Auriol also comes to visit. She is Dad's aunt on his maternal side, the younger sister of his wonderful mother, Hilary. Auriol is in her early nineties and, despite being the last remaining family member of her generation, is incredibly bright and active. Dad is her godson, and up until this point has been very involved in helping with her affairs, visiting often, and getting her settled into her new retirement home. She has relied on him, and now the roles are reversed and she is standing at his bedside, holding his hand, heart full. The visit is enormously emotional for Dad. I imagine that he must miss his mum, our lovely granny. An extraordinarily kind, unflappable, endlessly supportive woman who brought up five children on top of catering for a whole boarding house of teenage boys on WW2 rations. Auriol represents an older generation from whom one might seek support and reassurance; who will help to calm and contain your fears; who will tell you it will all get better.

Auriol smiles beautifully at Dad for the entire visit and it is only in the car, on the way back to her retirement home in Worcester, that she reveals she didn't hear a single word he said. The journey should take just an hour and fifteen minutes, but I manage to go completely the wrong way. This is the kind of thing that Dad would get into a flap about, if he knew; my driving, my questionable sense of direction, careering along like an unguided missile. Auriol is an impeccably polite passenger, sitting with her handbag perched on her knee, never commenting on the fact that I add an extra hour to our journey and take us through villages she's never even heard of. When we get there (eventually), we have a cup of tea in her room. I notice a little silhouetted portrait of a child on her wall: a child in adult's clothes. She tells me that it is of an ancestor of ours called Herbie. For some reason, this tiny discovery cheers me up. Herbie. I've never heard of him. I love the name. I drive home, the right way this time, but am exhausted when I get there.

Authenticity
15 September 2013

I'm heading into London today for a meeting with Jim O'Hanlon, the director of episodes 1 and 2 of *In the Flesh* series 2, which I will start filming in two weeks. I'm wearing Mum's vintage Jaeger coat, which I'm hoping will distract from my tired eyes. Before I leave, Mum and I have a big heart-to-heart. I say to her that I sometimes don't feel 'real' enough. I feel like I try too hard to be cheerful and positive when I don't actually feel that way. I force it, and then end up feeling exhausted. This lack of authenticity is starting to bother me. Mum reassures me that I don't need to try so hard. I set myself the challenge of being more honest and make Mum promise to do the same. I mention the fact that she apologised to me for not having tidied the house before I arrived! Dad's illness is bringing what is important into focus. I'm keeping in mind a quote from *Beautiful Ruins* by Jess Walter, which I have just finished reading: 'Do you mind if I speak frankly? I just don't have time not to say what I think any more.'

Good Nick
You're a good Nick.
But you're not in good nick.
And yet a good Nick you are still.
The very best and noble
Nick.

Slogan Hotpants
17 September 2013

Dad is so much better today. He is chirpier and more positive. He got really pissed off with Mum for trying to give him some prune juice to help with his bowels. It was a relief somehow; it showed some character. In my attempts to focus on what's important, I've realised that I don't need much in terms of clothes. I'm going to try really hard to shed things I don't need and have a capsule wardrobe. A well-thumbed copy of *Take a*

Break magazine from 2011 in the hospital visitors' room has some much-needed answers:

1. A cluttered wardrobe equals a cluttered mind.
2. Make a 'reality rail' excluding 'wardrobe monsters'.
3. Anything you haven't worn for two years – ditch.
4. Colour – can it be dyed?
5. Condition – shortened/lengthened.
6. Things to bin – gypsy skirts, batwing sleeves, anything shrunk or holed, slogan hotpants, old socks.

Although it is going to be a big blow, I feel it's time to let go of all of the batwing-sleeved slogan hotpants clogging up my wardrobe. I also desperately need a haircut.

An upbeat email from Mum to me and my siblings

> I've just taken Dad/Nick for a stroll outside to watch some charity abseiling on the next-door building. It was great to see him enjoying some fresh air at last! We then had a cup of tea in the café before returning upstairs. It was nice to feel we were doing something together for the first time in 3 weeks. Xx

The Bog
19 September 2013

Dad's main source of anxiety is something that used to be one of his great pleasures: going to the loo. He is completely preoccupied with it. This is an area of his life that used to run like clockwork (generally after breakfast with a copy of *The Times* sports section) but which now has become the focus of all his fears and frustrations. It affects the way he thinks about everything: what he eats, drinks and the timing of our visits.

In order to go to the loo, he must ring a bell and then get winched out of bed onto something called a Sara Stedy, a large plastic chair on wheels, on which he can then be transported up the ward and into the bathroom. He gets privacy once he's in there, which is a small mercy, but the anxiety lies in all the details that accompany it. What if he suddenly needs to go to the loo and the nurses are slow to get to him? What if someone else is in there? What if he can't go when he has the opportunity and has to return to bed unsuccessful?

We are lucky that the nurses are incredibly efficient, patient and good-humoured. Dad definitely needn't fear asking, but he finds it hugely anxiety-inducing to have to rely on other people for something so spontaneous and personal. It's difficult seeing him worried and distracted and it is hard to reassure him. It can also be frustrating when 'bowels' dominate the conversation. We joke about it in order to stay sane. I even write him a little limerick:

> There was a man famed for his rowing,
> whose preoccupation was 'going'.
> When he went to the lav
> and success he did have
> the nurses were all a bravo-ing.

This whole experience is rooting me in reality, in the present. Pulling me into myself in a way that must be positive. I don't yet know what the next chapter is, but when I do, I hope that this one will make sense.

Dadmin

21 September 2013

Dad is a bit distant, lethargic, and always tired. He got confused about what happened to him. What have I got? What's the game I've been playing? What's that? (It's an iPad.) We're worried that the light from his iPad is affecting his sleep, and are thinking about taking it away from him, but it feels cruel to do so.

A heavy feeling. The weight of the situation has landed on my chest, making me breathe more deeply. Reality is kicking in. I pray Dad's confusion is down to a UTI and not another bleed.

Frustratingly we don't yet know what has caused his stroke. So far, the CT scans have been inconclusive due to the excess of blood on the brain, so we're awaiting an MRI next week. We're worried that the stroke could be related to his renal cancer but try not to dwell on it too much.

Instead, we take it a step at a time and quickly get into a routine. I start each day the same: getting up early, trudging with Boris along the laboriously muddy canal towpath near our home, returning to make porridge and a mini-cafetière of coffee. I enjoy the simplicity of my morning activities and find them strangely comforting. Perhaps because they are reliably repetitious, or maybe also because I'm trying to fill Dad's shoes and that helps me feel close to him. I do a bit of ironing and generally potter and faff: cleaning surfaces, stacking random pieces of papers into piles, straightening things out, channelling my anxiety into small domestic tasks. I sometimes even tidy Mum's room for her, making her bed, folding and hanging her clothes, which she leaves strewn about the place. This might seem like a bit of an odd thing to do, but she is always too tired to do it herself, and it makes me feel more in control to feel that she's in control. We have lots of people to reply to, updates to send and phone calls to make. There is so much to do, day to day, that we coin the term 'Dadmin'.

Word has got out of Dad's misfortune, and we receive dozens of loving letters and emails every day. They come from friends, colleagues, ex-pupils, family members – all urging him on (mostly with some kind of rowing terminology that eventually wears thin). We read them out to him and his face pours with tears. It is like cartoon crying, where the tears shoot out vertically like water from a sprinkler. He cries and cries and cries. We debate whether he is crying in a positive way because he is touched and comforted or crying because he is sad. We fight about this because we all want to do the right thing by him and never know whether to go on or to stop.

The visiting hours are between 2 and 8 p.m., so between Mum, Oli, my big sister Kate and me we try to cover as much of that time as possible. We do an early shift and a later shift. Mum normally does the evening shift, coming in with a nutritious home-cooked meal for him. This is particularly decadent on Sundays, when Bevan Catering carefully decants all the elements of a roast meal into a thermal container, transported into hospital wrapped in a pristine floral tea towel. A kind of home-made Deliveroo. Even in hospital, Mum's standards for entertaining remain high, and she keeps a basket full of china mugs, Twining's English breakfast tea, fresh milk in a jam jar and dainty biscuits for any visitors who may come by. She brings a little bit of Mill Cottage to his bedside. She is being incredibly strong and is also completely at home on the ward, slotting straight into her old vocation as a nurse. She plumps

Dad's pillows, tucks him in, brings him fresh pyjamas, fresh pillowcases that smell of home. The last task of the day is helping him to brush his teeth, wash his face and hands, brush his hair, and generally get him as comfortable as possible.

Mum is determined that he will recover. On the first night in hospital, when she was told by the registrar that Dad would never walk again, her first thought was 'you don't know my husband'. It takes up every second of her day, every ounce of her energy. She has almost forgotten about herself; she has lost her appetite and is channelling everything into him.

Ebb and Flow

22 September 2013

Keeping a journal is helping me to look after myself. A sort of friendly page. I'm emailing Leo a lot. Sending thoughts, observations and music back and forth. I pour a lot of energy into this exchange, clinging on to it as something bright and hopeful. I am feeling strangely inspired and creative and I'm trying to mine it. Writing everything down. Appreciating the opportunity to lighten the load – or maybe just distract myself.

I am preoccupied with things. The things that surround me – photos, pictures, books, clothes, jewellery – all give me a sense of self. I'm someone who can't relax until her environment is 'just so'. (When I was a child, my parents had to endure many *Changing Rooms*-inspired makeovers in my bedroom. Always wanting to push the boundaries of my creative talent, I was constantly repainting furniture or engaging in haphazard cushion-making on my sewing machine. I imagine Mum and

Dad lived in fear of being gifted one of these bespoke cushion covers and having to display it in their smart coordinated sitting room. Perhaps the pinnacle of my young interior-design career was pinning a limp sheet to the wall above my single bed with a drawing pin, to create a makeshift 'safari chic' mosquito net.) In the hospital, I am repeatedly struck by the fact that all Dad has now is a small pine cupboard and a functional wheelie table that sits conveniently over the bed. His study at home is full of personality, teeming with books and memories and photographs. But this is a whitewashed, impersonal world. He has an iPad, toothbrush, toothpaste, mouthwash, sachets of green tea and some books. That's all.

In my daily scribblings, I am reminded of something I read once about an apple tree: bearing fruit for others but fertilising itself at the same time. I nurture my imagination and allow comforting thoughts to bubble up.

Mind Wander
Let's go for walk together.
In your mind you will feel the warmth of my hand through my imaginary glove.
There is a crew on the river.
And as we tire, Cassius Clay will offer you a seat beside him on a blanket under a tree. He'll say, 'Remember me, in British Honduras, NVB?'
I know you're having a bad time, but you're a fighter, he'll say.
You'll be OK.

Dad met Muhammad Ali in Belize on 24 July 1965. At that time, Dad was a captain in the British Army and was stationed out there with his regiment. Ali, or Cassius Clay as he was then known, had been visiting to put on a public exhibition match at the Palace Theatre. That evening Dad was out having a few beers in a bar, and after popping to the gents, he returned to find his seat taken. Politely tapping the man now occupying the seat on his shoulder, he was amazed when up from the chair rose the great boxer himself, a good three inches taller than Dad, apologising profusely. This was a wonderful stroke of fate, because throughout his life Dad had always been passionate about boxing. As well as participating in a bit of schoolboy boxing himself (from which he had obtained a wonky nose), he had also listened clandestinely to the big fights on a wireless that he and his brothers kept hidden under their school beds: Floyd Patterson, Ingemar Johansson – all the greats. Needless to say, Muhammad Ali stood for everything that Dad admired: sporting prowess, courage, charm and kindness.

I feel nostalgic for the old Dad. It's comforting to think about him as he was before; the little details that make him the individual he is, outside of the hospital bed. His enthusiasm for maps; his abhorrence of bananas, cucumber and cumin, which he pronounces as 'cummin'. His passion for peanut butter on toast, sometimes with marmalade or even Marmite. How, when I was a child and we went to the supermarket together, he would send me off on a covert mission to the patisserie counter, and we'd greedily eat our spoils in the car before driving home. How he'd draw mazes for us in the sand on the beach in North Wales. How he swam in the sea on Christmas Day. How he could conduct entire conversations on the phone with only 'yes' and 'no'. How he'd suck in his cheeks to make them look thinner. How he'd get all of his children's names mixed up and exclaim things like 'unwrap the fridge' instead of 'unpack the dishwasher'. How he always, irritatingly, won at tennis by playing on our mistakes. The way he liked his coffee: twice a day, once with breakfast, once after lunch.

Recipe for a Memory
1 teaspoon Alta Rica
And 1 teaspoon brown sugar into terracotta cup.
Add hot water.

Stir.
And let the memories fill your nostrils.

Jumping Ship
23 September 2013

Since the spring of 2011, I have been living on a spacious Dutch barge in arguably one of the most idyllic locations in London. Moored between Putney and Wandsworth, on a broad stretch of the River Thames, *Peregrine* is truly a thing of beauty. A vast industrial shell with endless soft hidden corners. The summers on deck have been idyllic, the winters a little more challenging, as she requires a lot of love, oil, diesel and coal. Within her steely embrace, I have never been so happy (or on occasion, so cold). I wake up in the morning to the shudders and groans of the tide coming in, to cormorants fishing and calling, to the steady familiar sound of oars patting against the water; constant cheerful activity. Back during the winter months, Dad would email regularly, wanting to know if I was warm enough afloat, asking me about my 'coal situation'. His interest in the boat came from a vast well of parental concern, but also, perhaps, from a place of envy. His life's great passion was rowing. He spent years of early mornings disturbing the river's waters and cycling its towpaths, loudhailer balanced precariously on his knee. He had a gift both as an oarsman and a coach. He was, it was often said, inspirational.

He came to stay with me on *Peregrine* once, when he had a rowing dinner in London to attend, and sent me a message utilising his much-favoured capital letters for emphasis, saying that he was looking forward to it 'HUGELY'. His one concern: 'How will I get back in when I'm drunk and it's midnight or will you be in town and can we return together?' It gave me great pleasure to play host to him. I noticed, when he came to drop off his bag, that he laid out his folded pyjamas on the pillow and put his slippers by the bed, ready for his late return. The sight made my heart burst a little. Perhaps because it was a nod to his orderliness or maybe even a glimpse of his vulnerability. Regardless, I took a photo of it.

I came to *Peregrine* as a temporary stopgap two years ago. Months turned into years, and I have been very fortunate to live here for so long. As I am about to start filming series 2 of *In the Flesh* in Manchester, it makes sense to move out of London and back to my parents' home in Oxfordshire. This way I can base myself with Mum and visit Dad in hospital as often as possible.

The weekend before the big move, Leo comes to stay. Since Berlin we have been emailing, messaging and Skyping, sharing music, poems, ideas, thoughts. He has helped me with my situation but also distracted me from it, because our rapidly intensifying daily contact has been something I've really looked forward to.

We had bid farewell in a dark corner of Berghain at about 4 a.m., and now meet again in the starkly lit surroundings of

Clapham Junction station at 4 p.m. (It's like being transported from a dreamy, softly lit indie film to a public information video.) An awkward time of day, 4 p.m.: too late for lunch, too early for a drink. 'Cup of tea, Leo? Welcome to London!' I am nervous about seeing him again. He appears, and I'm reminded of how handsome he is, his eyes a piercing blue. Like a lot of German men, Leo is tall and wolfish, with an intense gaze that peeps out from under a flop of dark brown hair. He is relaxed and easy, immediately taking control, and suggests, 'Shall we eat something?'

We spend three days together on the boat. We talk about everything, share everything. It is exciting and easy and sometimes a little bit exposing. He is unlike anyone I've ever met before, and I enjoy the way he sees things. He is the first person who tells me I'm an artist, and that feels significant. Nothing, I guess, feels more intimate than being 'seen'. I catch myself in various moments, and notice that it burns a little when he talks about his ex, with whom I think he is still in love. In a weird twist, one of the reasons he is in London is to collect some artwork that they had painted together. He goes to collect the suitcase of canvases one afternoon, and then lays all the artwork out on the floor between us, looking at it sadly. I try to act detached and bohemian in this moment, projecting an air of Patti Smith, but in truth I feel a little foolish.

And then, before I know it, we are at Clapham Junction again, this time bidding goodbye. We arrive early and buy him a salad in the station café, which he accidentally leaves behind. When his train pulls in, I kiss his cheek and leave the platform quickly. I wish, like the salad, this encounter had been left as it was.

Room 5
25 September 2013

Dad has been moved to Witney Community Hospital today, where there is a dedicated Stroke Recovery Unit. We're hopeful that he will be better occupied and challenged here, with specialist staff on hand for support, and physiotherapy in both the mornings and afternoons. After nearly three weeks at the John Radcliffe, we all welcome this change of scenery, and keep our fingers crossed that it will give Dad (and us) a new lease of life.

This morning, Dad was woken up at 8.30 a.m. and told that the ambulance was on its way. He is still waiting to be picked up at 1.30 p.m. We eventually get an anxious call from him on a doctor's phone at Witney Hospital at around 3 p.m., asking if anyone is coming in to see him. He laments that if he had his own mobile phone he could have called us himself. His trusty old Nokia is now defunct, and we realise that an urgent priority is getting him an iPhone.

Witney Community Hospital is much smaller than the John Radcliffe, and is positioned right in the centre of town, a few minutes' walk from a cinema, shopping centre and busy high street. You don't have to pay for parking here, which is a welcome change, and it's an easy half-hour drive from home. Dad has been given a bed in Room 5, which is positioned right at the far end of the L-shaped ward. A stroll through any hospital is always an assault on the senses; an ever-changing kaleidoscope of faces, smells, sounds and sights. It's hard not to glance into the other wards as you pass by and take in the state of the other patients. It is often a depressing sight. A stroke is such a cruel blow to the body, and I am reminded that in some ways we are lucky. Although Dad is paralysed down his left side, he still has his speech faculties, his face isn't too sunken, he has regular visitors and is very well cared for. It is not always the case for others.

Dad later tells us that he has been listening anxiously for our arrival, waiting for the unmistakable sound of our footsteps. When we appear in the doorway, we are full of smiles and enthusiasm, akin to a group of partygoers about to jump out and say, 'Sur-priiiiise!' We expect him to be thrilled to see us, but instead of greeting us with a warm, welcoming smile, he frowns, sending his one functioning arm shooting up into the air as a warning, aggressively mouthing 'shhhh'. It is as though we are a gaggle of schoolchildren who are late for assembly and being ushered in quietly by a disapproving teacher.

His new room is much more intimate than the large airy one he was in before. There are only four beds, two on each side. Dad is furthest away on the right-hand side, next to a large window. It becomes clear through a series of gestures that Dad is paranoid about disturbing the other gentleman in the room, Alan, who is in the bed diagonally opposite. From Dad's behaviour, you'd think that Alan was some kind of terrifying murderous dictator, rather than an amiable middle-aged man quietly engaged with a sudoku. We dutifully tiptoe past Alan, over to the bedside of Captain Stresshead, who continues to gesticulate wildly, begging us to speak in hushed tones and not make a fuss. For a good five minutes or so we stand around as still as possible until he is satisfied that we are behaving ourselves. Then finally he speaks, in a laboured *sotto voce*, slowly filling us in on the details of his first day, and the names of the staff that he has met so far. We all incline towards him like penguins, craning our necks to hear.

*

We help to get his things organised and settled as quietly as mice. Any bang or sound makes him anxious. He is clearly reluctant to draw any attention to himself. I can imagine shades of a young Nick, when he first went to boarding school: fearful of being teased, learning who he can trust. The change has been incredibly tiring for him. He is having to start all over again: getting to know the names and faces of the new nurses, the idiosyncrasies of the new hospital and its routines, his new room-mates. It must be very unnerving. In his anxious state, he has ordered the safest meal known to man: a jacket potato with cheese. We help to cut it up for him, mixing in the little pots of butter and Cheddar and adding a dollop of Marmite on top for some extra flare. (This quickly becomes a regular favourite on days when Mum doesn't cook.)

The most exciting piece of news is that Dad thinks he has felt some sensation in his left buttock.

Read-through in London

27 September 2013

Today we have the first read-through for series 2 of *In the Flesh* in London. I am obsessed with the fact that I look perpetually exhausted at the moment, so on the way to the read-through I panic-buy some miracle concealer that I hope will somehow erase the bags that seem to be taking up permanent camp beneath my eyes. Given the fact that my character in the show is a zombie, this is ironic. I'm not sure if it makes any difference, but it helps me to feel a little more confident as I enter the hot, packed-out room. Read-throughs are nervy, buzzy, caffeine-fuelled occasions. It is an opportunity to gather together the cast and crew around a huge circle of pushed-together tables, where we all introduce ourselves and, most importantly, hear the scripts read aloud – in full. (This is particularly useful for actors who have previously scanned through the scripts, looking only for their character's lines, ignoring everything else in between.) There's generally a snack table set up in the corner, where people congregate, nibbling on complimentary biscuits or croissants, anxiously waiting for it to start. People from production mill around, repeatedly reassuring the nervous actors that it's a 'safe space', that no one is judging anyone's performance, and then afterwards will come up and tell you in private that you did a 'great read'. Usually an executive producer or director will get up and do a big rallying battle speech to get us all excited that 'this is going to be a *great* series'.

It is famously hard to know how to pitch your performance at a read-through, whether to really give it some welly or be more understated. Read-throughs are especially nerve-wracking when you only have one or two lines to say, so you spend the entire thing in fearful anticipation, anxiously turning pages until you get to your one tiny line, which you blurt out far too loudly in a panic. Thankfully, my character Amy has lots to say, and as this is the second series of the show, I have the benefit of having been able to find my feet the previous year.

The atmosphere after the read-through is one of excitement and optimism. Afterwards, I get ushered off to have a costume fitting with the French costume designer, Yves, who as usual is wearing about three scarves tangled up together in an effortlessly cool knot around his neck. He gives me different combinations of vintage dresses, cardigans, belts and coats to try, and his team take lots of photos. The photos will be sent to the director and he will choose his favourite looks. It's a joy to be back in Amy's wardrobe again. The read-through and the fitting make the job feel much more real. We are actually doing this.

OCTOBER 2013

Trashy Bras and Hospitals
4 October 2013

Tonight is my last night on the boat. My dear friend and boatmate Issy and I drink a little whiskey and take in the most spectacular sunset over the Thames; a cloudless blue sky, sinking into a golden horizon, making the water shimmer bronze. The distant city looks hopeful, like a tangled string of fairy lights. I'm wearing some animal-print underwear from Ann Summers that is as cheap as chips but somehow cheers me up.

Lying on my bed, words now tumble out of me. I fill up page after page with, 'His home is Bay 5c. A muddy towpath walk is now a dream, a fantasy. My tongue sits so heavy. Body immovable. He is incongruous in this sterile place. A life marked down, reduced. His chamber cruelly broken open and looted. After seventy years. He looks like a majestic sea creature, beached and broken. Well-meaning nurses smile. Change shifts. But he remains. Immovable.'

Trashy Bras and Hospitals
Under muted ironed clothes
a layer of despair.

Cheaply made, rashly bought
Ann Summers underwear.

A vital need. A private voice
that wants to stay alive.
Beneath the beigey camouflage
my vital organs thrive.

I want you to revive.
To lift your silver hair
and comb you back into reality.

Polite well-mannered good girl.
Your friend and child.
But I'm not so good, Dad.
And I'm hating this, Dad.

I send you a cheery update.
'Have a great time, Em,' you reply.
And it's the worst message I've ever received.
Not even a rose
can bring you joy
in your plastic hell
where the smell of Mum's hair
is replaced by a curtain
and her gaze by
a stranger's stare.

I don't know how you can drink the coffee
out of those brown plastic cups.
Kissed by a thousand sorry lips.
You can't feel my hand. But I can feel yours.

Prosecco-swilling Nomad

5 October 2013

I have moved all of my belongings into an apocalyptic storage unit with the help of my friend Tors. It was liberating to lock away all of the stuff I've accumulated over the past few years, and to generally lighten my load. I'm now finally back at my parents' cottage in the middle of Oxfordshire, with its matching pale blue gate and front door, and delicately curtained windows. My room is small with a single iron bed and an antique chest of drawers that belonged to my grandmother. It is not *my room* as such, as my parents moved here after my elder siblings and I had all left home, but it's the room in which I always stay. I have only a couple of large suitcases to my name and they take up the entire floor space. Unpacking feels hopeless, so I'm now sitting in Dad's study, surrounded by his bookshelves and oars, my nostrils full of the unmistakable aroma of our Labrador, Boris, and the odd waft of roasting chicken, which drifts in from the neighbouring kitchen. I have a glass of Prosecco in my hand, which is lifting my mood, sip by sip, and clean, newly dried hair. I feel human again (just in time to return to the undead). The move, and the accompanying dust, is no longer sitting on my skin.

Dad is 18.2 miles away, but his portrait hangs over the door, just beneath a mounted set of antlers. The portrait was given to him when he retired as headmaster of Shiplake College – it's a depiction of him in his study: suited, animated, glasses resting in both hands, his expression gentle, open. The antlers were from Dad's first, and last, stalking holiday with my uncle Tim, where – as a complete novice – he shot a royal stag. A royal stag has twelve or more points on its antlers (six on each) and is seen as a great prize. Dad was reassured that the stag was old and wouldn't survive the winter, but despite this he felt very guilty about taking its life. He described making eye contact with the animal, weighing up the enormous responsibility in his hands, his heart in his mouth.

Today's Dadmin has revolved around Oli setting up a new iPhone 4s for Dad. This is the product of weeks of research and emails between my siblings in which I have been pretty unhelpful, beyond contributing my share of £17.50 towards his new handset. Everyone has sent photos and ideas for some new apps to entertain him. Dad is texting us now with his one functioning hand, which is a new and exciting development.

Mum is originally from Melbourne and we are very touched that some of her Australian friends and family have gifted Dad his own iPad. Up until this point, he has been using Mum's, and it has truly been a lifeline. He plays the game Words with Friends – a kind of digital Scrabble – all day long, competing against his siblings, children, wife and a handful of friends. He has even opened himself up to random international opponents, sending instant messages to them saying things like, 'I've had a strok. This is grt therapy. I'm in Oxford. Where are you?' One kind opponent replies, saying, 'My husband had a stroke. I'll pray for you.'

Network Error
6 October 2013

I am off to visit Dad today, for the first time in a week or so. With moving out and some pre-shoot rehearsals in Manchester, I haven't been able to be around. According to the rest of the family, last week was incredibly tough. Dad has been unsettled and low. They have all struggled to keep their spirits up.

Visiting time isn't until 3 p.m., so I have a number of messages from Dad before I go in.

> Any chance of bringing some nail scissors when you come ins.

> I have a therapy session this afternoon so don't come too early and ask to join in if I'm not in my roomxxx

> Dear em im getting network error on this machine when playing chess etc it says go to settings and reconnect but there isn't anything in settings that helps any quick ideas before yo visit

I'm anxious as to how he will be, but I find him in pretty good spirits, all things considered. He's wearing a new set of clothes that I've never seen before: a blue polo shirt and a grey sweatshirt; comfortable and practical. He has lost weight, unsurprisingly. His white hair has grown much longer than normal and softly curls up behind his ears. It suits him. As it's a nice day, I wheel him out of the ward and down to the modest but cheerful paved hospital garden with its little beds of red, cream and pink flowers. Dad doesn't really notice the plants (very unlike him) and is utterly focused on his new iPhone. It's like hanging out with a teenager.

My first line in series 2 of *In the Flesh* is: 'Sad. Nervous. Excited.' It couldn't be more accurate. I am due to start filming in two days' time and am feeling sick with nerves. This is something I go through before starting every acting job, my system flooded with adrenaline and fear of the unknown. Fundamentally I just want to do a good job and do myself and the story justice. Mum is amazing when I get like this and has come to expect the 'anxious-Emily-starting-a-new-job' phone call. She reassures me by rationally pointing out that I always end up loving my work and the new people that I meet and will probably ring her again in a week or so sounding on top of the world.

When reflecting on how to approach playing my character, Amy, something that is very much at the forefront of my mind is the fact that she was institutionalised for a long time. She battled against leukaemia and was robbed of her health, her autonomy, her youth, and ultimately her life. Like Dad – a person with huge ambition and energy confined to a hospital bed. Amy and I are, in general, very different. We have in common an ability to appear outwardly confident but to paddle quite hard under the surface. She is *far* bolder than I am, hugely demonstrative and wears her heart very much on her sleeve. (My own heart is more zipped up somewhere hidden.) And yet for me, this distance between us gives me space to run and play. She jumps off the page and into my bones. Playing her feels like the most natural thing in the world. Dominic Mitchell, the writer, sends me a text.

> Keep the light and shade of Amy alive. She's not just a sidekick. She's her own person with full access to all emotions, including the bad ones.

Before I leave for Manchester, I get an email saying: 'Kate wants you to see this purchase on Amazon.' My big sister has bought me an iPhone charger and plug, having heard from my brother Oli that all of mine are broken. 'I heard about the ridiculous situation from Ol and decided to take matters into my own hands.' She knows I'm broke and unorganised, and this is so, so kind. Crucially, it enables me to stay connected to home while I'm gone.

First Day
8 October 2013

Unit Call: 4.30 p.m.
Estimated Wrap: 3.30 a.m.
Weather: A dry but cloudy night.

First day back on *In the Flesh*. Night shoots. As I wait in the hotel foyer to be collected at 15.30, I feel a strange mixture of excitement, dread and nerves. I savour every moment of the long car journey through the Lancashire countryside, glancing occasionally at the annotated script on my lap and muttering lines to myself. The very first scene I'm going to shoot is described thus: 'Amy stumbles towards the farmhouse.' I think I can just about manage that. We drive for around an hour and eventually arrive at our location, which is on a hilltop in Ramsbottom. It feels like we're in the middle of nowhere. I relish the experience of getting ready in my trailer, shedding my skin and pulling on all the various pieces of costume that transform me from Emily into Amy Dyer. I pull on thick tights, two huge petticoats, a vintage tea dress, chunky cardigan, waisted belt, long black patent boots and some bright retro jewellery. The multiple petticoats create such volume that they bounce around me as I walk, rising and falling. I feel incredibly comfortable, which in turn makes me feel confident.

In the makeup truck, all of the colour is slowly drained out of my cheeks, little delicate veins are brought up, and the signature swampy, bloodshot, pinprick pupil contact lenses are placed in my eyes by a specialist to complete the look. This is the moment that completes the transformation, because not only do I look very different, but I *feel* different too: strange and 'other'. I'm reminded of this constantly by the way people genuinely jump a little when they see me. 'It's the eyes!' they say, shivering slightly. The occasional unit driver braves, 'I've woken up next to a few like you, love.' The intricately decorated contact lenses are vast and purposefully so, in order to cover the whole eyeball. Luke Newberry, who plays the lead role of Kieran Walker in the series, likens it to sticking a pair of teacups in your eyes. Getting them in is perhaps the worst part of the job, and we have a specialist on hand to do it for us. You have to sit back in the makeup chair and try to relax, avoiding thoughts of the time you had to go to Moorfields Eye Hospital with a scratched retina, while your eye is prised open and they are forced onto your eyeballs. At best they feel scratchy. We try to keep them in for short periods only, giving the eyes a break. I can't see very well through them, so it is like a veil has been drawn over me and the world becomes muted. Darker.

After makeup, I sit on the sofa in my little trailer and go over the scenes that we're about to shoot, reminding myself of where we're at in the story, as we never shoot in chronological order. One of the scenes we're shooting is a zombie rave and I am going to be high on 'Brains!' (sheep brains in lieu of eating human brains).

When it's time to go for rehearsal, I get a knock on my door, and a lovely new runner takes my arm and escorts me over to the set. As we walk across to the barn where the rave will take place, the sight of Manchester twinkling in the distance is utterly magical. I feel a lightness in this vast expanse that I haven't felt for a while. The nerves have now turned to excitement, and I just feel very lucky. This is a welcome distraction from what's going on at home.

Jim O'Hanlon has tons of energy and enthusiasm and shouts, 'Listening now, listening!' before the camera starts to roll.

Normally the last thing you'd hear before a scene would be the first assistant director shouting for silence, then, 'camera rolling', 'sound rolling' and 'action'. 'Listening' is a simple but great note that immediately sharpens up your senses and brings you into the moment.

We're shooting seven scenes tonight. I manage my first stumble towards the farmhouse without any hiccups, and then I shoot my first scene with Emmett Scanlan. It's exciting to work opposite him. After that we film the zombie rave, where I bound up to Luke, high as a kite on sheeps' brains, grabbing his cheeks, kissing him and throwing a neon band around his head. We are surrounded by a room of hipster undead, pretending to dance to music that isn't actually on for sound-recording purposes. Luke and I have to throw our voices above the imaginary hubbub. Working with him feels like the easiest thing in the world. Since series 1, he has become one of my closest friends and we trust each other implicitly.

Back in my hotel room at 5 a.m. I take a long, spaced-out bath. I'm buzzing from a brilliant first day. I email Leo telling him all about it. The new crew and cast have brought in a wonderful injection of energy, so hopefully we're on track for a great second series. Alarmingly, I only know what happens in script 1 and 2. I might get killed off...

Worrying Symptoms
11 October 2013

I chat to Emmett about what is going on at home and his eyes fill up. He is clearly a devoted father to his own daughter, and I can see he is pained by the idea of what we're going through.

It's another occasion where I can read the seriousness of my situation in other people's faces. I remain strangely emotionally disconnected when I describe everything that has happened. I guess I have to be for self-preservation – especially in the workplace. It's weird that as actors we are instruments of emotion, and yet maybe only playing with a certain set of notes?

About an hour before we wrap I read an email from Leo that makes my stomach turn. It would be impossible for anyone to tell under the layer of pale makeup, but I can feel my cheeks drain. After he came to visit we have been in touch every day, several times a day. It has been pretty intense. Mum has been worried about me locking myself away every night for our deep chats on Skype, concerned that I don't have the energy for it, but I've ignored her. I've loved the connection. I've sent him poems and songs, and he has sent me films, and little bits of writing. He gives me a note to 'throw away my pretty girl's dress, and allow my voice to be more wanting, needing'. So I do just that – and send him something that I had written after he had left the boat.

I cannot bear to look at this poem, even now, five years later, which gives you an idea about how bad it was. Really bad. Always keen to please, I had duly obliged. I had thrown my sweet floral dress onto the floor (why, Emily, why?) and slipped on my black cloak of truth. No, worse than that, I had thrown that off too and stood there in the hopeless, metaphorical, poetic nude. I didn't even lighten the tone with rhyme. Oh no. I did however throw in a reference to risotto (we had eaten risotto), and there was some kind of reference to a knife being twisted. And something went 'thump' on the floor. My pride?

It is unflinchingly honest and he is hurt and shocked, not wanting to have made me feel like that. A bit burned, I think. Wondering how we can go forward after this. This is after him saying to me a few nights ago that I'm the closest stranger he's ever met. Over the course of the next few days, we try to patch it up, but everything unravels. And from me, a whole mess of emotion and feeling is expressed and exposed. I know it's too much, but I can't keep it in. My heart is all over my sleeve and on my shoes and in my hair and trodden into the carpet. The connection between me and Berlin strains, snaps and is broken. Another power supply cut off. Line dead. The end of my first week of filming goes out with a bang.

That night, Luke comes to the hotel, and we order large glasses of red wine on room service. I cry on him and decide to text a psychic line. They tell me repeatedly, 'You need to focus on yourself.' That is the last thing I want to do.

How Much for Your Knickers?
12 October 2013

Saturday morning. I pack up my bag and make the short walk to the train station. I'm not needed until Tuesday, so will have a good stretch of time with Mum and Dad. In a perverse twist, as I'm walking out of the hotel, trailing my suitcase, a man jumps out from behind a hedge and asks, very politely, if he can buy my knickers.

Yesterday's Knickers
'How much for your knickers?' a random stranger says.
How much for my knickers? 'Yes. Yesterday's.'
How much for yesterday's knickers?

Blue, I think. A touch of pink.
I mean I'm not terribly attached to them and depending on how
much he gives me
I could buy a nice new pair of knickers; ones that actually
match my bra.
He's twitching now.
Thrusts a pair of someone else's 'yesterday's knickers' into
my sight.

Yesterday
they were today's knickers.
Chosen from the crowd in all their silly frilly
knickerbocker glory.
Carefully unfolded.
Teased from toes to the tip of the thigh.
Held in the most private of places.
Then cast aside.
Used.
Unclean.
Just a part of routine.

He wants them.

Today.

Just as they are.
He can have them for free.

I go straight from the station to the hospital. My first visit with
Dad in a week. He is very tired and a bit blue today, and because
I'm feeling quite low and a little wiped out myself, it is hard to be
upbeat for him. I should be coming in with fresh energy to buoy
him along, but I'm flat as a pancake. He's really concerned about

his phone numbers being transferred onto his new phone. I'm awful at this kind of thing. I wonder if we should simply email everyone, saying that Dad now has a new phone and would love to hear from them. It's a frustrating visit. He is preoccupied, as always, with his bowels. Going to the loo is without question his most pressing concern. It must be awful to have to rely on other people to take you to the bathroom. Even worse to have to be transported there on the Sara Stedy. I find I don't have the patience to talk about bowels today. I think the night shifts have taken their toll a little. I don't stay for too long, which seems to suit us both, before heading home and going straight to bed.

Identity
A black sugared coffee
and a pale and milky tea
made me.

Sunday Church
13 October 2013

I go to church with Mum for the first time in a while and realise that the prayers that have long been lightly pencilled in my mind now feel more urgent. I have sat between my parents for years of chapel and church services, and know their every nuance, emphasis and change of key. But here, in our cold little village church, it's just Mum and me in a pew that is too big for us, and the script has changed. A little boy gets up and reads a big worldly prayer in a small voice. I shut my eyes and make a wish. The vicar says, 'He is yours. Yours and mine.' Oh God.

Among a drizzle of parishioners, I sit. Words seal the deal. I want to believe this.

Reality Bites
14 October 2013

With my bubble burst, reality bites. I realise that Leo has been a kind of analgesic, buffering me from reality. I experience new, painful waves of feelings about Dad. I think I have been distracting myself and it's like a plaster has been ripped off. I think about all the times that I have felt hurt or hurt people before; it bubbles up like bile at the back of my throat. Fuck, it hurts. It happens, it happens. I try to remain positive but I feel a bit out of control, like the balance has been tipped. I feel like everything has started spilling out over the sides and I can't keep it in. It's bubbling up and I'm not sure which bit tipped it over the edge. I wallow in London Grammar. My notebook is full of fragments. I try to find a narrative that will make it all OK. I feel so many things.

Daily Scribblings
14 October 2013

I
haven't yet found
a picture to
fit the frame

Loose Screw
Made of solid love,
So securely built,
unbreakable each part.
Then, set along the rocky path.
The remote control only lasts a few metres,
then you're on your own, kid.

Don't wage a war on your insecurities.
Change the rules.
Raise the bar.
Start the car
and drive where
you
want to go.
You've got wheels.

I want to believe this I want to believe this I want to believe this.

Poetry and Lyrics
15 October 2013

I chat to Jim about the fact that I write poems and songs, and he tells me the theory that poetry can exist on its own but lyrics need to be married to music in order to be whole. He tells me to listen to Leonard Cohen, so I spend the evening soaking in the bath, blasting out 'Suzanne' (which I love) and scribbling in my notebook.

Poetry
Like a diary entry.
A simmering down of wordy stock
into something strong and smooth
that you can taste.
An experience or an emotion
captured
and frozen into word-shaped moulds.
Painting in raw technicolour.

I appreciate the sterility of being in a hotel. The space, the orderliness, the faceless neutrality of the place in contrast with the messiness of home and my chaotic inner life. It's a little bubble world, entirely for myself. I can get lost in long dark corridors, surrounded by ever-changing faces.

Hotel
A blank domestic canvas in plum.
Your home in a room.
No air in here
but you will survive on tea and shortbread,
hairdryer, remote control and kettle at your side
and a fresh pen for every fresh thought.
And if I spill the virgin ink
someone invisible will bleach it away
along with any trace of me.
I have baths and showers and baths because I can.
The art matches the curtains, matches the carpet, matches the
pillow, matches the pen.
White sheets
pulled tight across the bed like a fake grin.
I shall listen to TV in the shower and dream of breakfast.
All the comforts of no one.

Daily Scribblings
16 October 2013

I
baked an ache overnight
and awoke an hour and a half late for life.
Must eat some nuts and bolts of lightning will occur.

Today I...

1. Woke up early and got up late
2. Washed my hair and dried it straight
3. Ate two eggs
4. Called Mum
5. Went to an art gallery
6. Learned about class and industrialisation
7. Walked around a new part of town
8. Bought a kilt
9. Ate breakfast for lunch
10. Spoke to a stranger in a chocolate shop
11. Wrote a postcard to a psychic
12. Read a newspaper

Something

about his fingerless gloves made me want to...

She

so wanted him
outside her window
breath steaming glass.

'You get me'

Does that really mean: I'm the only person who can tolerate you

Doctor's Surgery

17 October 2013

Today we're filming scenes in the doctor's surgery. Amy is frightened about her strange symptoms, so comes to see a doctor about her tremors. I'm wearing my favourite costume for this series. A pink floral tea dress with a dark rose-pink cardigan with dark berries and leaves embroidered on the shoulders. A little brown leather bag slung over the top, and a butterfly necklace, among other trinkets.

Dawn Smooths the Mind, Like a Brush Through Knotted Hair
23 October 2013

I'm back home with Mum for a few days and it's good to be here. The filming is going well, all things considered. I'm really enjoying working in the expansive Yorkshire Dales and being blown about by the elements; it feels calming and life-affirming. At home, too, I relish being close to nature, especially my morning walks with Boris. Poor Boris. His once-regimented routine has been totally turned on its head. Dad was devoted to him and walked him early each morning and most afternoons for ten years. Now he looks confused at his demotion, picking up the scraps of people's time. My circadian clock has become attuned to 5 a.m. alarm calls, so I wake up early and am happy to get out onto the canal with him at that time of day. It's misty and magical; I enjoy breathing the fresh air into my lungs and stretching out my legs, resetting the system. Mum heads to the hospital at lunchtime, and while she's en route I receive an email from Dad, who is having technological issues. His iPad – or 'this machine', as he refers to it – is desperately important for his quality of life. Playing chess, or Words with Friends, or reading *The Times* online are distractions that help to fill the long hospital hours between the excitement of mealtimes, physio, loo trips and visits. In his pre-hospital 'retirement' life, Dad's days were packed full of meetings, coaching, courses and a bit of golfing. There was very little time for sitting down for long periods. He's certainly making up for that now.

> Dear em I,m getting network error on this machine when playing chessetc it says go to settings and reconnect but therein,tanything in settings that helps any quick ideas before yo visit?

> Sent from my iPadtrying to grt the times it says please check your internet connection and try again!

I reply with:

> Hmm. Interesting that you can send emails. Maybe try shutting chess down and opening it again? You remember double clicking the button on the side. And then sliding up your finger to shut applications. Try that and then opening it again. Xx

I then get two emails saying 'connected thanks'. I tell him that I'll be in to see him at 4.30/5 p.m.

Before leaving for the hospital I decide to leave Mum some crispbreads as a snack to try and ensure she eats something. (Is there any foodstuff more dry-sounding than 'crispbreads'?) I also leave a note explaining what else needs doing and end up leaving a little later than planned. When I eventually get to the hospital at around 5.15 p.m., Dad's face is furrowed with concern about my driving. What would happen if I crashed? Do I know where to find the insurance details? For every agonisingly long minute after 5 p.m. he has clearly imagined increasingly worse consequences.

*

My driving has always been a source of concern for my father. I'll never forget how utterly astonished he was when I arrived home one day, jubilant after having successfully passed my driving test. The process of learning to drive had taken two tests, four instructors, as many years, and a little chunk out of the wall in Reading Station underground car park. My first test had been brought to a close prematurely after I drove the wrong way around a roundabout, leaving my poor examiner visibly shaken. By some miracle, in my second test, the driving gods were shining down on me and I got through unscathed, much to the amazement of my awaiting instructor, who practically dropped his flask of tea. As soon as I got home, I picked up the keys to my Peugeot 205 (small, but with the gravelly baritone of a tank) and lurched off down the road to Henley, where I was so pleased with myself that I forgot to pay and display and promptly got a £40 parking ticket.

Years on, Dad is still anxious about my driving. I eventually manage to calm him down and we have a good chat, catching up on the days that I've missed. He loves hearing all about my job, and the people that I'm working with. He's told all the nurses what I'm up to and is keen to introduce me to one of them, who is an *In the Flesh* fan. Dad is as curious as ever to know how it all works, particularly the geography of where we've been filming, so we spend a bit of time on Google Earth zooming in on a rural train station, among other places. We had an amusing cameo this week from the playwright Jim Cartwright, writer of *The Rise and Fall of Little Voice*. He does the odd acting job for a bit of fun and is hilariously patronising as the station officer who refuses to sell Kieran a ticket because he's 'partially deceased'.

I've brought some of Dad's art materials with me today and suggest that we do a bit of drawing. Dad really took to art in his retirement, and our house is full of his paintings. In the early days, he was less concerned with us liking his artwork, anxious to know that we simply recognised what it was. He once showed me a picture of what was quite obviously a welly boot and said, 'What's this?' When I replied correctly he was absolutely delighted. Less successful was the very nice picture of a river, which wasn't actually a river, but in fact the road outside our house.

Today, I encourage Dad to try to draw his left hand. I imagine it might help his brain to connect to it, in a similar way to his daily mirror-box therapy. Dad draws his hand, on my request, and then gets bored and starts to draw me instead. I can tell by the mischievous expression on his face that what he's drawing is far from flattering. Out of revenge, I start to draw him too, and it is equally bad, though I enjoy studying his face. He has a sloping, skew-whiff smile. His face looks handsome, his cheekbones sticking out more because he's so much thinner. Afterwards I chop up some Golden Russet apple that I picked from the garden and give it to him in little chunks. We agree that it's like feeding a tortoise.

I trim his fingernails. He jokes about me doing his toenails too and we laugh heartily until I realise he's serious. So I pull off his socks and tend to his toes, finishing off by massaging hand cream into his poor dry feet. It is difficult to comprehend that he can only feel it on one side, no matter how hard I pummel his left foot. I think we all live with the hope that we will miraculously bring back some kind of sensation – some little pin or needle that we can cling on to for hope. But no luck. Regardless, it's satisfying to make him more comfortable, and he is so grateful. Perhaps the intimacy of the foot rub has relaxed him a little. We talk about his anxiety. He is anxious all night, unable to sleep with the worry that he'll need to go to the loo. It seems helpful for him to share this with me, although I can't offer him much in the way of advice. He says that I am very understanding and that he is glad that he can talk to me about these things. I really try to connect and listen to what he says. Hold on to each important word. They are precious.

I think a lot of actors are very sensitive – sensitive to people, to situations, to moods. I think so much. I sometimes want to put my head on standby.

Royal Academy Australia Exhibition
24 October 2013

Mum, Oli and I plan a day out together, starting with a trip to the Royal Academy to see the Australia exhibition. The exhibition itself is wonderfully nostalgic for Mum. There are a number of her favourite masterpieces, including Frederick McCubbin's ambiguous triptych *The Pioneer*, and *A break away!* by Tom Roberts. I bulk-buy postcards in the gift shop that, as usual, I will probably keep rather than send to anyone. We head over the road to Fortnum & Mason to indulge in our favourite treat of a Welsh rarebit and a glass of fizz (from Cornwall). The setting in Fortnum's is beautiful, light and elegant. The waiting staff are in immaculately pressed aprons and appear faintly Parisian. Our absent Dad pays for lunch, wanting to do something nice for us all. It's good to try and do something 'normal' together, but it feels slightly strange to be in this beautiful place. We are all quite anxious and talk about Dad a lot.

A Very Sad Thing to Say

25 October 2013

I go over to visit my sister Kate, who lives half an hour away. It's also an opportunity to catch up with my niece and nephew, Maia and Toby. Toby, five, says, 'I've got a very sad thing to say.'

'What's that, Toby?'

'I haven't been able to see Grandpa yet.'

Later that day I email Dominic Mitchell, writer of *In the Flesh*.

> Dom just to add another message because my last one was fired off all too quickly in the hospital. Dad and I were looking at old letters today which means that messages like this on a phone feel crap, but I cannot tell you enough how lucky I feel to be playing this role in *In the Flesh*. Out of all the roles in all the world in any programme, this really is my dream. The best. To be amongst such brilliant people who make me raise my game every day, and with your extraordinary words which are the beginning and end of it all. I'm feeling all sentimental so you have to forgive me but it really is the most amazing gift. Xx yours with mega appreciation for making it all possible xx

NOVEMBER 2013

Doctor's Note
1 November 2013

Dear Dr Ranger,

I hope you are well. We were wondering if you could help us with something.

Subsequent to my father being admitted into hospital, a number of bills arrived for him that were unopened, and thus weren't paid for some time. Therefore we have incurred a number of fines.

It is possible to get a refund if we present the companies with a doctor's note, and we were hoping you might be kind enough to write one stating that Nick has been in hospital since 2 September.

He presently remains in Witney and we are awaiting results of an MRI and various CT scans to see how his cancer is progressing.

Best wishes,
Emily Bevan

There Isn't Going to Be an End

4 November 2013

Mum, Ol and I go into the hospital today for an important meeting with Dr Warner, who has overseen Dad's treatment at Witney. He has got the results of some recent brain scans. We anxiously wait by Dad's bedside, and he tells us that his heart is pounding. Soon Dr Warner comes into the ward and calls us into a small room. He has big eighties hair, a whiff of Status Quo, and a kind manner. Also in the room is a South African nurse and a rather handsome young doctor whom I try not to consider to be handsome in this situation. He makes notes throughout and seems entirely disconnected, which jars a little with the emotional charge in the room.

Dr Warner speaks softly and carefully, explaining what we had perhaps suspected – that the bleed in Dad's brain was caused by his renal cancer spreading to several places in his head. With his working hand, Dad gently taps the side of his head and says something like, 'In here?' to which Dr Warner replies, 'Yes.'

Throughout all this, Mum holds Dad's hand, which is bound up in a supportive splint. She rubs it and holds it tightly, even though Dad can't physically feel it. Dad is incredibly brave throughout. After we all ask some questions, the medical team leave us alone to have a moment together. We all burst into tears instantly. Mum keeps rubbing Dad's hand and kissing his head. Oli takes the other hand and I'm left with his legs, which I try to hold and hug reassuringly. We laugh through the tears at the absurdity of the situation.

Through sobs, Dad keeps saying, 'There isn't going to be an end. I can't see an end. Just more hospitals.' He really cries, like he did in the early days. A huge physical release. He also says, beautifully and optimistically (so like him), that he had been convinced it was going to be *good* news.

And then apologised to us for all the bother.

I don't think I've ever loved him more. We don't know what to do, so once we've recovered ourselves a little, eyes wiped with the sleeves of jumpers and many breaths exhaled, we decide to get outside and go for a walk. We dress Dad up in his black cashmere polo neck, Nicole Farhi gilet and blue woollen scarf with the pink-spotted silk lining. He looks so handsome with his combed silver hair and blue eyes, which seem brighter somehow, still glistening a little with tears. We wheel him down the corridor, and as we pass the physiotherapists he apologises to them too for missing his session.

We walk around the cold hospital car park for a while, before deciding that the Marks & Spencer café is the place to go and contemplate life. Our cold cheeks flush as we enter the jarringly bright and festive store, and we push Dad through stacks of Christmassy tins, bright festive jumpers and other premature Christmas paraphernalia. We eventually make it to the lift and take him up to the Sparks café.

I offer to get the drinks for us all, and stand queuing for fifteen minutes, infuriated by the wait and silently channelling all of my grief and frustration towards the painfully inefficient barista. When I glance back at the table at my stricken family, I can see that Mum's eyes are red raw. We're all winded by this news. Eventually I take the tray over and we sit with our drinks: coffee for Mum, Oli and me, and a green tea for Dad. In the past he might have opted for a hot chocolate in this situation, but he won't touch them now. He is so sensitive to his digestion, he just wants to drink clean liquid. He seems calm, but tells me off when I try to fill the silence with something positive wrapped up in rowing terminology. This is fair enough. There have been endless encouraging rowing comments and he's completely fed up with it. There are just no words.

We stare searchingly into our disappointingly milky flat whites, where there has been an attempt at artwork in the foam. I add sugar, stirring, hoping for an answer. We barely have a few sips of our coffee before Oli and I have to leave to get to the station; me for Manchester and him for his teaching job in Oxford. More mumbled frustration about the barista. We accompany Mum and Dad back to the ward, say our farewells and then head off together.

When Oli and I say goodbye, we both agree that we feel OK but will probably cry again when we're by ourselves. Interestingly, Alain de Botton's tweet today, glimpsed literally as I went into the hospital, was:

> 'Dealing with death,
> we either have to
> look it squarely in the face
> and nothing makes sense,
> or repress it and carry on'

We have to carry on.

Oli and I decide that a good thing for us to focus on is Dad's memoirs. He had actually started writing them himself a year or so earlier, entitled 'Early Recollections', and is keen to try and complete them. Dad is a wonderful storyteller, and despite everything that is going on, regularly has us, and himself, in fits of giggles. We have some memorable afternoons recording him, as he softly and carefully retells stories from the past to the regular metronome of his heart monitor. It's wonderful hearing some of these stories for the first time, and amusing to watch Dad deliver them to us as if he were dictating to a secretary, clearly and slowly, finding the right words and the right emphasis.

In these moments, Dad is occupied, distracted from his anxiety, and seems more content. The plumped-up downy pillow that Mum has got him is so deep and soft that it occasionally threatens to swallow up his entire head, encasing it like a wimple. He leans over when he is speaking, to draw us in.

It's interesting what stories bubble to the surface from his long, full life. These stories have lodged in his memory as clear as day (I can't even remember what I had for breakfast). There are recollections of formative years at school. The story about a boy who was being so badly bullied that he took himself up to the school clock tower at night, where he slipped and fell. How it sent ripples through the school and Dad never forgot it. The 'scouting exercise' at Abberley when Dad and his friends were sent off to a place called the 'Valley of the Rocks' to find a teacher who was pretending to be dead, and how they couldn't even lift him onto a stretcher. Another was about the time his brother Tim fell over and broke his nose when showing off, running along a row of beds. Dad laughs and wheezes so hard telling this particular story that I worry we may have to send for a nurse.

These recordings are interrupted with the occasional 'ooh, my back's sore'.

A Memory of Abberley
Weekends at Abberley
were long
and slow

but

made
so much better

by our nearby grandparents

who were wonderful hosts to us.

Bearing in mind one was never allowed out for the day one was
only allowed out for a meal

But having them nearby made a huge difference.

At one stage I was ill... and... with a...

with a swelling on my neck

which had to be operated on.

And my mother was able to come over and stay with them
while visiting me in hospital

which would not have been easy for other parents.

The Valley of the Rocks
One vivid memory
                is of
                      a scouting afternoon
                              when we solemnly paraded
              and um

        and the scoutmaster failed to appear.

And we were a bit concerned.

And eventually summed up the courage to go to the common
room – a smoke-fugged place

        which – we never went near

Knocked on the door and said
        'Mr Hughes hasn't come for scouts.
What should we do?'

and the

        chaps inside put down their pipes

                    and

suggested we went and looked in 'The Valley of Rocks'.

So sure enough,

a couple of dozen
                boys
sprinted off

to 'The Valley of Rocks', which was a big trench
I suppose about fifty feet deep
in the woods

Quite dangerous!
                    And
                    um
Definitely out of bounds.
            We went off there

I think I went first along the valley floor
        two others went along the top of the valley
                and suddenly there was a shout from one of the
                observers on top!
                'There's a body!'

And sure enough very rapidly we came across the hapless Mr
Hughes covered in blood and clearly severely injured.

Or was he?

            This was in fact a clever ruse.

                    But a very good exercise for us young lads.

It only broke down when
                Having sent for the stretcher
                                        we were
Twelve of us
        Quite unable to lift him off the ground.

We could hardly get him on to it

Let alone off it

Um.
Anyhow.
It all ended happily
Um.
End of story.

Fingernail so

> **From:** Nick Bevan to me
> **Subject:** Fingernail so
> **Date:** 09/11/2013
>
> Hope you're home safely coild you possibly do my nails when you come ins? And I'd love mum to have a da off if at pall possible
> Xxxxdad.

An Email Update to Family and Friends

Dad is vague, confused and complaining of headaches. It's scary, as we fear he could have had another brain haemorrhage. We send an update to family and friends.

> 17/11/2013
> Dear all,
>
> I'm so sorry we haven't been in touch with an update sooner. We have had an anxious time waiting for the results of Dad's latest scans, and it has now been confirmed that renal cancer was the cause of the stroke. He will soon begin treatment for this, beginning with a

short burst of radiotherapy.

In terms of his mobility – a new exercise bike routine is proving very effective and is bringing out his competitive spirit! He suggested that he and a few other patients should try to notch up the miles between Oxford and Cambridge. When the occupational therapist cheerfully announced that they were 'getting near to High Wycombe', Dad smiled sweetly (but was secretly appalled at her poor sense of direction).

He is still in hospital in Witney and has even managed a few emails from his new account. All correspondence is very welcome, but please don't be offended if he doesn't reply, since he finds typing one-fingered difficult and the physiotherapy leaves him tired. If the physio goes to plan, our hope is that we will get him home in time for Christmas.

We all send love and as we've said many times (and we really do mean it), we are hugely grateful to everyone for their tremendous support.

The Bevans x

22 *November 2013*
I got back to Banbury last night after a delayed six-hour journey from Manchester, and found Mum in a complete state about Dad. This isn't a surprise, because when I left earlier in the week I was also very anxious about him. We crept into the ward to say hello on the way back from the station and got to spend about ten minutes together. This was totally outside of visiting hours, but Mum has become so close to the nurses that they

make these allowances for us. Mum is extremely worried and tearful, and I reassure her that I'm here, and will stay with her this weekend.

A poem that I read to Dad*
I shared a moment with the world.
Spent a moment with a view.
Standing in an empty field I bled my heart out
to the cotton-wool sky and I felt so small.
So tiny a speck,
so insignificant a life.
No heartbeat for miles, save the curious sheep.
Suddenly so free.
The world and me.
I marched up her back to admire her contours better.
Like sneaking into an artist's panorama.
I sang to her.
Loudly.
I danced in my heavy muddy boots.
I could see for miles. The dead tree. I, blown, balloon-like, by
the wind.
West. North. East.
Lost and unseen among the gradients of green.

*He is fairly nonplussed but likes the bit about 'gradients of green'.

Dad is having a very low week. This has been made worse by the fact that his physio told him he would never walk again. Kate and Oli are furious about it. His physio is quite irregular anyway – and now this. Even if it's true, I don't think they should say that to people – how is it helping?

An Awful Day
26 November 2013

Dad has to be taken back over to the John Radcliffe Hospital today to have his head measured for a protective mask that he will wear during his radiotherapy sessions. With any cerebral tumours, the pressure on the brain can cause headaches and sickness, which movement can exacerbate. Poor Dad is already feeling sick before setting off, so the nurses inject him with something to help with the nausea.

On Dad's insistence, Mum drives directly to the John Radcliffe Hospital to meet him there, rather than accompany him from Witney. Dad's ambulance doesn't arrive at 5 p.m. as planned, so by the time he arrives at the John Radcliffe they have lost the appointment. The specialist agrees to fit Dad in at the end of the day, but this means another three-hour wait.

Mum sends updates from the hospital. She tells us that the journey in the ambulance has left Dad feeling incredibly nauseous, and that he is now actually being sick. It is awful for both of them. When they finally see the specialist, Dad has his mask fitted, and we learn that he will start the five-day radiotherapy treatment on Wednesday 11 December, finishing on Tuesday 17th. She then says, 'Seven to ten days later he'll lose his hair and will possibly have a sore scalp. What a shame this coincides with Christmas. The sooner we get out of 2013 the better!'

Eventually the ambulance comes to pick Dad up and take him back to Witney, and Mum tells the ambulance crew that Dad is feeling really sick and to please drive *very* carefully and slowly. The driver says, 'Don't worry. We'll look after him.'

The ambulance drives so fast back to Witney that Mum can't even keep up. When they open up the back of the ambulance, Dad is covered in sick. Mum describes the scene as 'horrific' and is incredibly upset that he has been all alone in the back of an ambulance in such a sorry state. The wonderful nurses at Witney are shocked to see him, and sweep in to clean him up and get him comfortable. One in particular keeps saying, 'Ooh, Nick, I can't let you out of my sight.' The most troubling thing is that Dad then starts to experience a horrible sensation of falling backwards, and has the dreadful feeling that something awful is going to happen to him. He's frightened that he's going to have another bleed.

He never travelled by himself after that.

DECEMBER 2013

Love by
6 December 2013

> Dad: Good morning am very worried about you driving in this weather so please be careful of
> Love by

> Me: I'll be there at 2 p.m.

> Dad: L no worries no hurries amp

> Dad: All
> Slept s little better at
> Last now feel exhausted after shower.

> Me: Oh Dad. Well one positive out of two isn't bad. Great that you slept better. That will give you a much better day today. Tiredness from showers is only temporary I'm sure! Looking forward to seeing you later xxx

Legs to Stand On
9 December 2013

Dad has been signed over from the stroke physiotherapist to the head of physio at Witney Community Hospital, Lou. I think she's taken him on as a special case. She is a very energetic lady, almost ageless, who wears shorts even in December and oozes with the can-do attitude of a PE teacher. We've been feeling quite disheartened about this area of Dad's treatment, but Super Lou has come along and managed to get Dad to stand without a great deal of effort on her part. She teaches him to lift his bottom off the chair and then to use the power in his core, and one working leg, to stand.

All of this week, she manages to get him up on his feet twice a day. Mum is invited to join Dad on his second gym session and is incredibly impressed by Lou's ability to instil confidence in him. Dad's goal is to be able to move from the wheelchair into the car. Mum writes to me in an email: 'Walking can come later, but if Dad can get into a normal car it will greatly enhance his independence (and mine).'

Oli has been teaching Dad to record voice notes on WhatsApp, rather than send texts, in the hope that it will be easier for him (and his thumbs).

Voice note from Dad to me, 8.55 a.m.
Oliver's been showing me a
New
System
For
TEXTING
I hope it works I hope you get this I'm looking forward to seeing you.
Um. And um
I'll
I'll ring off now,
But you might JUST send a text back saying you GOT it.

That would be very kind.

Lots of love.

Voice note from Dad to Mum, 11.01 a.m.

While you're at the hairdresser,

when you're...

when you've *finished*

could you

possibly buy me a

very SOFT

hairbrush

suitable for the top of my head when I've

gone bald (nervous laugh).

Um...

I think it'll be....

and

when it's... when its *tender*

I think it'll be very helpful the current hairbrush I've got is

far too TOUGH

A Small Voice Coming from Upstairs

12 December 2013

Approaching Christmas, it has become very cold and our spirits are quite low. Putting aside for a moment the emotional and psychological strain, there is also the exhaustion of driving back and forth from the hospital, at least one or two return journeys each day. Oli and I have work as a distraction, but Mum doesn't ever have a day off, so we insist that she must stay at home for once and have some time for herself. She does this reluctantly. I try to persuade her to book a massage, but she is very firm about the fact that she doesn't want to and that a massage *wouldn't be relaxing.* When I get home from the hospital in the evening, I open the front door and am greeted by Boris, sleepily wagging his tail and rubbing his head against my knee affectionately. I call Mum's name but hear no answer. I open the door to the sitting room and call again, picking up the faint sound of a small voice coming from upstairs.

I find her moments later, fully clothed, standing in the bath.

Poor Mum. She was boiling some potatoes for supper (her favourite) and while carrying the saucepan from the hob to the sink, the old plastic handle broke and the saucepan and its contents went all over her. She was wearing thick socks because it was so cold and now has one very wet, very hot, stinging foot. Her nursing instincts kicked in, and she took off the hot sock and ran upstairs, filling the bath with cold water. She has been standing here for half an hour to prevent her foot blistering and would have stood here longer had I not got home and found her. All she is thinking about is that she cannot get out of the bath because she will get a blister, and if she gets a blister, she won't be able to drive and thus go and visit Dad. I eventually lure her out of the bath and into a bucket of water which sits under the kitchen table. Miraculously, no blister.

Mum
You are so pretty, Mum.
So pretty.
I wish I'd told you often because I've thought it.
And I thought you knew.
Look at you – feet burnt, standing in the cold bath.
I felt such tenderness for your ironed jeans.
Your short legs
that carried you

ten thousand miles from home.
I'm writing this on a piece of paper
torn from your scrapbook.
I, your 'piece of paper' girl
with the same tired eyes.
You are so pretty, Mum.
So pretty
and I wish I'd told you often because I've thought it.
And I thought you knew.

Kill Your Darlings

19 December 2013

We have now completed filming the third and fourth episodes
of the series. While I've been away, I've kept in touch with Dad
a lot through WhatsApp, sending him pictures and little hellos.
He got grumpy with me at one point for sending him a photo
of my hotel breakfast just after we'd finished talking. 'Hi Em, I
thought we'd already been in touch?' He's tired.

After we wrap filming, I am returning to my trailer when the
producer John catches me and asks if he can have a little chat.
Inside my trailer, and comfortably seated on the tiny leather
sofa, he announces that he's got a bit of news. There have been
rumours going around the set that something quite dramatic is
going to happen, plot-wise, and he wants to let me know what it is
before I read the script. He tells me that at the end of episode 6,
Amy, my character, is going to be fatally stabbed.

Even though we are talking about a fictional character, someone
who is a construction of the writer's imagination, she is also
now a part of me. I find this news really quite painful to hear.

Perhaps even a tiny bit hurt that it could be happening to us
(Amy and me). I smile and say that I look forward to reading
the scripts: they are hot off the press and sitting in my rucksack.

On the journey back from Manchester to Banbury, I devour the
final two episodes and it is a brilliant and devastating read. The
tragedy comes at the end of the series, when Amy is stabbed
to death by MP Maxine Martin , of the 'pro-living' political
party, Victus, just seconds after feeling her heartbeat for the
first time. Needless to say, I'm pretty emotional by the time I
get home. I don't want to tell anyone about what is happening
to my character, as it will give too much away when they see the
series, but I do confide in Dad, who seems quite thrilled to be
sharing the secret with me.

Radiotherapy
21 December 2013

Radiotherapy is a horrible and aggressive thing to endure and
leaves Dad exhausted and very sick. For the time being, he is
having to be winched out of bed to a commode rather than
being taken to the loo on the Sara Stedy. He is far from happy
about this, insisting that he can do it. But he's so weak and tired
that the physiotherapist is worried about him injuring himself.
The staff nurse, Cally, is very understanding with him and helps
him get to the loo as much as possible. He needs to rest. His
physio is cancelled until after the Christmas bank holiday.

A number of different patients have passed through Dad's
room. An elderly Indian gentleman who arrived with great
drama in the middle of the night, a painfully thin Irish jockey
and a tiny man who looked like a dormouse and had an

extremely high-pitched voice. In the run-up to Christmas a number of empty beds in the hospital fill up. We speak to the nurses about this, and they explain that it is common for people to check into hospital at Christmas time in order not to be home alone, and to get a decent meal. Oli is moved to see one such person pick up a whole jacket potato and take a huge bite out of the side of it, such is his hunger.

Ed and Debs
22 December 2013

We have a long anticipated visit from my eldest brother Ed, his wife Deborah and their two kids, Penny and Sophia. They are over in the UK from Dubai, and bring an injection of energy and warmth that is much needed. Little Sophia is not yet two, and runs around the ward seemingly oblivious to the hospital sounds and smells, beaming at everyone, smiling openly. It cheers all of us up. In the car on the way home, I teach Penny, twelve, a simple technique for writing a poem. You choose an emotion, and then go through each of the senses, describing it in turn. Happiness looks like, tastes like, feels like etc. A nice distraction.

The Carol Singers
23 December 2013

Having retired to a small North Oxfordshire village in 2004, Dad and Mum made it a priority to head up to the church on Sunday morning with the hope of immediately diving into the heart of the place and meeting like-minded people with whom they might become friends. Dad went up to the vicar at the time and apparently said, 'Hello, I'm Nick Bevan. How can I help?' Mum and Dad quickly found themselves enveloped in an incredibly warm community that centred around the little medieval church. Throughout Dad's illness and beyond, I learn that there is something immensely sustaining about this little sacred place, and the collective energy of the people who congregate there week after week. As a family we are well known to the current rector, Marcus, and the community of churchgoers. Until recently, Dad has been a part of the rhythm of the place, his voice mingling with theirs in the pews on Sunday mornings. In his absence, he is carried along in their thoughts and prayers and we feel their warmth throughout this ordeal.

And it is these people who come into the hospital on 23 December and bring the music of Christmas all the way to bay 5c. They stand just outside the door, so as not to intrude on him, letting their tidings of comfort and joy weave together and fill the space between them. It is the music of Dad's childhood; it is the music of hopefulness, warmth and goodwill and it breaks through, for just a little while, the bleakness of it all.

Faith Healing
24 December 2013

We receive an email from Uncle Richard, describing what an important influence Dad has been in his life. I reply to it saying:

> Dad and I have just sobbed our way through this. What a wonderful and moving and generous message. Dad is so touched and grateful. I'm replying on his behalf because he's very tired, as ever... Thankfully he hasn't been sick

in the last few days but is just hugely fatigued. So this is from him, via me.

Carols from King's is on in the background, which he's finding very moving. He mentioned that your uncle Edward used to have a regular pew?

Yesterday, some very kind friends from the village came into hospital to sing carols for Dad outside his room. Oli texted me from home saying, 'Have there been enough tears to sink a hospital?' – and he was pretty accurate. Dad is so touched and moved by people's care for him.

Mum, Oli and I are coming in tomorrow at 12 for our £8 turkey dinner! Starting with prawn cocktail! They're kindly setting us up in the day room here, so we can all sit around a table.

Kate and Charlie will join us later on for presents.

Thinking of you all and sending lots of love and huge thanks for your very very kind words. I can't do them justice in response.

Xxxx

When it comes to religion, Dad is certainly a man of faith, although he sometimes confides that he isn't *exactly* sure what he believes in. His brother Tim, and many other people, describe him as being 'good'. A good man. Kind. And selfless. He carries a lot, gives a lot, and never asks for it back. In this way he encompasses the essence of Christianity.

But faith – as we could call it, or God – has without question given Dad strength, something to lean on at moments when there has been nothing else. When my brother Oliver was born, he was critically ill, and taken immediately to a life-support machine after swallowing meconium. Mum will never forget the moment that a doctor got into a lift with them and casually said, 'Mr and Mrs Bevan? Your son has a fifty-fifty chance of surviving,' and then got out of the lift. They were absolutely desperate, helpless, and all Dad could think to do was go down to the chapel under the hospital, hold hands and pray. They poured all of their energy into it. The hospital rector, who later became Oliver's godfather, got Mum and Dad to visualise Oli with a halo around his head. And that day, he started to get pinkness back into his cheeks, and they genuinely felt a miracle had occurred.

Christmas
25 December 2013

Christmas has been very quiet, but precious. Oli and I hid a stocking in Dad's locker last night, on Christmas Eve, so that he would have something to enjoy and open in the morning. Sadly it didn't get discovered by the nurses, who are no doubt run off their feet.

We come in at midday, and the ward is all lit up and looking very bright and festive. This morning I hurriedly printed out lots of pictures of Boris and stuck them onto some pieces of card, so that Dad could give us all a Christmas card. While Oli and Mum are out of the room I hand him a pen, and he hurriedly scribbles us all a little note. This has become my most treasured possession in the world. Mine reads 'Dear Em. You are absolutely wonderful and I love you for it xxx'

The nurses have very kindly arranged for us to have our own private Christmas lunch together in the day room. They want to help us achieve some kind of normality. We all dress up for the occasion. Mum is wearing a blue velvet dress, her peacock pearls around her neck, and Dad is in a pale blue checked shirt and maroon cashmere gilet. He has lost a lot of weight, and his grey hair is very soft and thin. He hasn't worn a shirt for months, and his neck pokes out of it like a tortoise from its shell. His Christmas hat perches on top of ears that look too big for his head. He hasn't got any appetite but eats a few morsels to be polite. It's very difficult to see such an energetic and positive man so tired, unwell and frustrated by his paralysis. We try very hard to keep our sense of humour as much as possible and still manage to enjoy this moment together.

Oli gives Dad a brilliant book called *F in Spelling: The Funniest Test Paper Blunders*, which genuinely puts a smile on his face. I had gone to Hatton Garden, on Dad's request, and bought a pair of pearl earrings for Mum, from Dad, which she absolutely loves. We had discussed buying them a month or so before, and Dad had welled up, telling me that that '*this* Christmas I really want to treat her.'

For a family who have fairly high culinary standards, we find the NHS Christmas pudding to be a revelation; moist, comforting and delicious. We enjoy it with a healthy dollop of industrial brandy custard, and it is quite frankly one of the nicest things I have ever eaten.

After a little while, Dad is completely exhausted and wants to go back to bed. Shortly after, Kate and Charlie arrive with the kids, who manage to bring a smile to his face. They are so sweet with him; concerned, gentle and serious. He is a long way now from the Grandpa who would potter around the garden with them, giving them jobs to do, reading them stories, lowering his glasses on to the end of his nose and making silly faces. It is undoubtedly upsetting for them to see him like this but they are very brave, and get a good, strong, reassuring hand squeeze from Grandpa. After leaving the hospital however, Maia is worried that she kissed Dad on 'the wrong side'.

The last visit of the day is from Marcus, our local rector. It is bitingly cold outside, and quite hazardous on the roads, and it feels rather magical that he materialises out of nowhere, red-cheeked from the freezing air and festivities. These gestures of kindness, of people going out of their way for us, have never meant more. We pull the curtains round and Marcus gives Dad his very own private bedside communion. Afterwards, they pray together.

Each time that Marcus has visited, he has read out Psalm 139, the words of which Dad has grown to find enormously comforting. He cries every time he hears it (and so does Mum). Listening to it read aloud, it feels like an incantation to soothe Dad in his suffering. The words have a powerful effect on him and I can understand why. The psalm seems to be about showing yourself to God: opening your heart and allowing yourself to be known. To be held in his knowledge. I think the words of the psalm seem to reassure Dad that he isn't alone in his suffering. That he isn't going to be alone whatever happens. That he has nothing to fear because he has nothing to hide. God is 'acquainted with all my ways'. He is an open book.

Oh Lord, thou hast searched me, and known me.
Thou knowest my downsitting and mine uprising, thou understandest my thought afar off. Thou compassest my path

and my lying down, and art acquainted with all my ways. For
there is not a word in my tongue, but, lo, O Lord, thou knowest
it altogether.
Thou hast beset me behind and before, and laid thine hand
upon me. Such knowledge is too wonderful for me; it is high,
I cannot attain unto it. Whither shall I go from thy spirit? or
whither shall I flee from thy presence?
If I ascend up into heaven, thou art there: if I make my bed in
hell, behold, thou art there. If I take the wings of the morning,
and dwell in the uttermost parts of the sea;
Even there shall thy hand lead me, and thy right hand shall
hold me.

I think that, quietly, this psalm helps Dad prepare for what
might be ahead, although we still are totally in denial about
what that might be. We say goodbye to Marcus, thanking him
warmly, and then settle Dad in for the night.

Back at home, we drink too much Champagne to try and
make ourselves feel better. I pass out during *Downton Abbey*
and eventually crawl up to bed. Too tired to do my impression
of Cora.

New Year's Eve

31 December 2013

Partygoers across the country are raring up for a night of
revelry and merry-making, but around Dad's hospital bed in
bay 5c we are slightly lacking in fizz. He is still totally wiped
out from the course of radiotherapy that he undertook before
Christmas, which has left him feeling drained and nauseous.
Spirits are understandably low.

*

New Year's Eve is traditionally a night when Dad would cook Mum something deliciously retro from a well-thumbed Raymond Blanc cookbook. *Escalopes de veau à l'orange*, served with a French accent and copious glasses of Champagne. He was always very romantic, running her baths, lighting candles, making her feel spoilt, '*Che gelida manina*' blaring in the background. Tonight, the soundtrack to the evening is the steady metronome of heart monitors and the murmur of nurses going about their familiar routines. Mum has brought Dad roast chicken and gravy in her trusty Thermos, which she decants onto his NHS jacket potato. He hasn't got much of an appetite but is grateful, as always, for a taste of home.

After dinner we help him to clean his teeth, wash his face and hands, and comb his hair. I always find this bit quite satisfying, having become a bit of a connoisseur of the hot flannel (the only way to melt away layers and layers of thick makeup after a day's filming). I hope it helps to melt away a little of Dad's day too. I also enjoy brushing his hair, which is soft and fine, and almost perfectly white. Hopefully we leave him feeling a little fresher and more comfortable than before. Mum collects any clothes that need to be washed, and places newly ironed pyjamas in his bedside locker. She finds it hard to say goodbye tonight, but Dad is keen that we don't stay too long and go and have a nice evening. His bed is positioned by a large window, and as we linger before departing, holding his hand in farewell, we can see local fireworks exploding in the distance.

Neither Mum nor I feel like we're going to be particularly good company, but the effort is minimal given that we simply have to grab a bottle of Champagne from the fridge and walk thirty seconds over the road to our neighbour Jane's house. She immediately puts us at ease and we are grateful for the distraction of fun and lively company. Tomorrow I have tickets for an all-day party in Vauxhall where Âme and Move D are DJing. I have a restless need for a blowout.

New Year's Day

1 January 2014

I booked the tickets ages ago, and have persuaded Luke to come up from Devon to join me. I leave home optimistically, but as I travel up to Marylebone Station, and across London, weariness sets in. I meet Luke and we head into the club, which is uncomfortably rammed with people. It feels weird to be there in the early afternoon and it's just all wrong. We end up in the neighbouring Starbucks a few hours later having a granola bar and a festive latte. Not quite the day we had planned. Luke is totally relaxed about it all, which is typical of him. Thank God for him; he is the least judgemental person you could ever meet. As well as sitting by me while I've cried into large glasses of Shiraz (ordered on room service), he has also handed out wisdom beyond his years, distracted me and made me belly laugh. He's a true soulmate who I felt a connection to the moment we met in the chemistry read for series 1. The director, Jonny Campbell, had brought Luke and me together to read a scene from episode 2, where Kieran and Amy show each other their scars and reveal how they died. I remember doing the scene, and looking into Luke's huge brown Bambi eyes, which were full of empathy and warmth, and totally welling up. It's a gift to have someone close to you at a time like this with whom you can be completely authentic; and who, by some miracle, still seems to find you vaguely entertaining company.

A Stranger's House

I think I'm losing you.
But not carelessly.
When as a child I lost you
I felt the butterfly panic,
eyes searching strangers
until I found you again.

I have such a strong memory of being a little girl and coming out of a party onto the drive in front of a stranger's house, running full speed towards Dad with my arms outstretched and throwing myself around his legs, shouting, 'Dadddeeeeee!' The man looked down at me and said, 'I'm not your daddy.' I stared up at him, horrified, let go and ran away.

JANUARY 2014

Hold On
4 January 2014

Today, Dad squeezed my hand and quietly said that he didn't
know if he wanted to do it any more. 'It' being what? Life.
Radiotherapy. Treatment. Hospitals.

He's so tired. We had been clinging to the hope that once he
had gone through the radiotherapy treatment before Christmas,
he would finally start a new drug that is known to be very
effective for renal cancer. Before the stroke, Mum and Dad had
met a number of people at the cancer support group who had
done very well on it, and the plan had been for him to start
the drugs in October, once they got back from their summer
holiday.

Dad explains to me today that more radiotherapy feels like too
much for him to cope with. It would entail more ambulance
trips, more sickness, more discomfort. I stroke his hand and say
that I am grateful that he's shared how he's feeling.

In the evening, I go home and sit on the floor of Dad's study
with my head against his desk. I'm playing the guitar almost
every day at the moment. Strumming away and seeing what
comes out. I start with a chord (normally a melancholy minor
chord) and then add another melancholy minor chord, and just

sometimes, a song tumbles out effortlessly, perfectly formed, in a wave of pure emotion.

A Song for Dad
Hold on
when your fingers are slipping.
Hold on
keep your hands gripping
cos I don't know what to say.
There's no answer anyway.

Hold on
when your mind is swimming,
I'll swim with you there
our fingertips kissing
cos I just want to be there
where we go now
I don't care.

I know.
Sometime you have to go.

Don't carry me – you must just carry you.
I'll be fine now. I'll be fine now.

Don't carry me because I want to carry you. I am strong now.
I am stronger now. You taught me how.

Hold on. Hold on. Hold on.

Feeling Sick is the Worst
7 January 2014

This week Dad's appetite has dropped off, and he's still feeling nauseous and being sick. Feeling sick is the worst. And it is constant for him. When Dad's asleep, Mum is called aside by Dr Warner, the consultant in charge of the Stroke Recovery Unit. He is worried that Dad's cancer could have spread to another major organ, and that this could be the cause of the sickness. Dr Warner makes a fair point, but Mum is so upset by the conversation that she has to wash her face in the loo and walk around for fifteen minutes in order to calm herself down before going back to Dad's bedside. She doesn't want him to see her cry. Throughout their married life, Dad has always been carefully attuned to Mum's emotional state. Today, he is simply too exhausted to notice.

The idea of Dad having to travel anywhere is unbearable, but Mum is determined that he see the renal cancer specialist as soon as possible for a professional opinion. Mum is advised by the nurses that it's possible to hire a private ambulance. (This is a revelation to us.) So she sets up an appointment with the specialist and arranges for an ambulance driver called Russell to collect them in two days' time.

Back to Work
9 January 2014

Love
Love is taking up all the space in my room.
I've had to put some of it in the fridge
and under the stairs.
Unfortunately, it cannot be recycled.

It is very un-environmentally friendly.
Once opened you must consume the contents
even if it makes you feel sick.

I'm on my way back to Manchester to start filming block 3,
the final two episodes of series 2. It's very hard to leave home,
but thankfully I'm only needed on set for one day and then I
can return home again. I've left my car at the train station so I
can easily get home the following night. I'm thinking of Mum
and Dad so much and hoping that the driver Russell does
his stuff and that the journey is as painless as possible. Dad
and Mum are currently on their way to a private hospital in
Oxford for more scans and a meeting with Dad's oncologist. Is
Dad's nausea still being caused by the radiotherapy or is there
something more sinister going on? Hopefully today will shed
some light...

Getting on my train, I decide that a day like today warrants
an upgrade, so I head to First Class, stretch out my legs and
sit proudly, holding my £10 ready for the ticket inspector.
The luxury bubble is burst within about five minutes, when I
discover that upgrades are only cheap on the weekends, so I
decamp to the nearby 'quiet coach'. Luckily, I don't have much
baggage with me. Mum gets in touch to say that they got to the
hospital OK and that the ambulance was just like a normal one,
but more comfortable. Russell was apparently very nice and
helpful. Mum has tried to get through the day as tearlessly as
possible, but it has been a struggle. I suggest that she could try
counting up to ten repeatedly to calm herself down, something
my new Headspace app has been instructing me to do. I also
tell her that she should have a Pizza Express margherita from
the freezer for supper.

*

Meanwhile, I will be having tapas with the director of block 3 (episodes 5 and 6), Alice Troughton, and her director of photography, Dale Macready. As always, it's exciting to be working with a new director, and everyone has been raving about Alice since she started a week or so ago. Each new block, with each new director, feels like a fresh start. They bring an injection of new energy and insight and really help to challenge you and push you in new directions. My storyline really intensifies now, giving me the opportunity to play more with the light and shade of Amy's vulnerability – and mortality. Quite refreshing, actually. I suppose *I'm* feeling more vulnerable and serious too, so in some ways the two of us are helpfully in sync.

My (Almost) Death Scene
10 January 2014

I can understand why the reports about Alice have been so glowing. She has an extraordinary handle on our stories and our characters' journeys. She is passionate and energising.

The part of the story that we are filming today is pretty heart-breaking. It is the scene where Amy asks Philip, who has just become her boyfriend, to kill her, because she fears that she is turning rabid. She is desperately frightened of being out of control and hurting people again. 'It's a fate worse than death,' she says. The scene is set in a tent on a windy, rainy moor, which for filming purposes has been set up in the middle of a deserted warehouse. We do a quick read-through of the lines, but Alice doesn't want to rehearse too much, wanting to keep the intensity and charge as fresh as possible. I'm normally very chatty when I'm on set, but while they're setting up for the first shot, I take myself off to the corner of the room and nestle into my big warm coat (a practical, down-filled one, which sits over my Amy coat), and try to find a bit of quiet and focus.

At the end of the scene, just as Philip (played by the phenomenal actor Stephen Thompson) is about to bring a screwdriver down into her head, Amy realises that she can feel the raindrops that are falling on her face through a hole in the roof of the tent. The scene suddenly shifts from one of horror to one of rapture as Amy realises that she is, miraculously, coming alive again. It's beautifully hopeful. I finish the day feeling exhausted but on a big acting-induced high.

I manage to get home to see Dad this evening, and am shocked to discover that he has somehow become thinner and lost even more of his hair in the short time I've been away. We talk a lot about how the filming went. How nervous I was starting with a new director and DOP, but how lovely they'd been to me; how the work had felt really connected. While Dad and I are chatting, the staff nurse comes over and expresses concern to us about Mum. She explains that the road to recovery is long, and that if Mum carries on the way she is, she is going to burn out. This is a tearful exchange because Dad so needs Mum, and Mum wants to be there as much as she can. But we appreciate what the staff nurse is saying and agree to give it some thought. The next day, we agree that Mum should have a day off.

Mum's Day Off
11 January 2014

Mum doesn't agree to have the whole day off, but to *some* of the day off, coming in later in the afternoon. I head in at lunchtime, determined to hold the fort in her place. When I walk into

Dad's hospital room, I can see that he has been anxiously looking out for me and is crying out from an agonising pain in his chest. Coming to his bedside, I don't know what to do, so I just hold his chest, one hand on his back, one hand on his front. He has already been given morphine, Nurofen and paracetamol. Nothing is working. His eyes are scared. He is asking for Mum. He is also really thirsty.

I can't get him comfortable. He agonisingly coughs up the most awful combination of spit and blood that almost chokes him. It's awful to see him in such pain, and we're both tearful. His eyes are bloodshot. I just say to him, 'I'm here.' He can see that I'm upset. I can't keep up my defences in this moment and choke up when I helplessly say to the nurse, 'That was quite frightening.' Dad, through his own pain and fear, tries to reassure me, saying, 'I don't want to traumatise you, Em.'

I am acutely aware that this is Mum's day (or at least part day) off, and don't want to fall at the first hurdle by panicking, giving in and calling her up. The lovely nurses reassure me that it is nothing serious and suggest that I go to the local pharmacy in town and get some microwaveable heat packs to put on Dad's chest. I go off immediately and buy three of them. Dad also needs some cream for a large rash on his hand. At the till, I ask the pharmacist if I can buy two packets of the cream but they say that I can only have one. I am so upset and frustrated that they won't let me have two that I break down in the middle of the pharmacy, unable to form words, impotently trying to explain that I think my father is dying.

Back in the hospital, the heat packs aren't working. I ask that another doctor is sent for and keep holding Dad's hand. Mum arrives, very upset. She is so shocked to see how Dad is, certain that his excruciating pain must be pleural. Every breath is torture. Dad tells her that I've been brilliant but I feel like a total failure. I should have called her earlier. Mum then tells me to send for my brother Ol and sister Kate, and I am so upset and shocked at her suggestion that 'this is it' that I burst into tears again. One of the nurses comforts me outside the ward and says, 'Let's wait and see what the doctor says.' I speak to Ol and Kate and say I will update them.

The doctor comes to Dad's bedside and thinks that it's a chest infection. She taps his chest a lot and prescribes him some antibiotics, which he washes down with a few spoonfuls of a toffee yoghurt. The only thing he manages to eat today.

His temperature is high, so we put cool flannels on his head. I soak the flannel in a bowl of ice that we've been given and Mum snaps at me, saying that the flannel will be too cold. We are both taut with stress and shaken up, and at that moment I can't handle being criticised. Dad sees my hurt and Mum's desperate concern and tries to soften the atmosphere, saying that I'm only trying to help. Even in such enormous pain, he tries to be a mediator, to keep balance in the family. I love him for that.

Indignant, I take myself off to the family visiting room, where I promptly break down into floods of tears. I manage to calm down, and a short while later decide to head home. It isn't a particularly meaningful goodbye. It is usual for us to hand over from one visitor to the next and I feel that I need to get out of there. I can't even remember what I say, but I know that I need to go.

At home, I eat sweet-potato mash and fall asleep in front of the TV.

A New Script

12 January 2014

At 5.45 a.m. I wake up to hear someone saying my name outside my bedroom window. Delirious as I am with sleep, it sounds like a voice from God. In reality, it is Dave from up the road. He says, 'You need to get to the John Radcliffe Hospital now.' I see that I have a number of missed calls from Mum and messages telling me that Dad is in a critical state and has been taken to the JR.

I feel eerily calm and get dressed. Dave offers to drive me there but I say I'm OK. I get in the car and try to call Kate and Oli on the way. No answer, but it's still so early. I drive into Oxford in a daze, wanting to put on some music but unsure what to play.

In the emergency ward I am met by the duty doctor, who says that she has been expecting me. She is softly spoken and has intelligent, kind eyes. She says that Dad has been in the resuscitation unit but has now been moved. She takes me to a curtained-off room where Mum and Dad are. Dad is unconscious and being aided to breathe by an oxygen machine. His breathing is very laboured, and his cheeks are sucked deeply into the mask over his face with every inhalation. His chest rising and falling. Mum is in tears. I give her a big hug and we cry together, kissing Dad, holding his hands, all the while trying to contact Kate and Oli. I eventually get through to my sister but have no luck with Ol. I try phoning his housemate, Dee, who picks up immediately, and within half an hour he is in a taxi from his home in south London.

I ask the nurses if Dad can still hear us and if we should talk to him, and she says that we should. She says that his breath is slowing down now, which is a sign that he is getting ready to let go. The regular rhythm of his breathing gets noticeably slower and slower, and then there is an extraordinary moment where I just know, in an instant, that he has gone. I am holding his hand and I feel it. Something disappears, there is a change of energy, sucked out of the air. We kiss him and kiss him, tucking our hands under his neck, clinging on to the last of this great man's abundant warmth.

The ward is very quiet. It feels like we are the only family here.

When Oli eventually arrives, he says, 'Did I make it?' and I say that I'm really sorry but that we lost Dad about an hour ago. Such strange words to be speaking out loud. I'm worried about how he will take it but he too is incredibly calm. It grounds us, the enormity of this moment, like we're carrying something heavy and precious and have to step carefully, thoughtfully. It's like we're in a new world. It is a new script.

Kate arrives, calm, but forehead etched with heavy anticipation. All four of us stand around the bed for a while, going through a Rolodex of emotional responses. Disbelief, shock, pain, attempts at humour crumbling into helpless tears. We look at Dad and each other, and try to let it sink in. After what must be around an hour, a doctor comes and instructs us that she needs to do a number of official checks to confirm that Dad has indeed died. This seems extraordinary because no one could look more dead at this point, but it is important that they are rigorous about these things. While she does the checks, we are told that we can sit in the family room, a small human container in shades of magnolia and soft blue. Nothing too harsh or strong that might upset. Cups with saucers.

When the doctor has finished her checks, we individually go in to see Dad again, to say our goodbyes. I thank him – for everything – tell him I love him, and then have the strange experience of bidding farewell and leaving him there.

On the way back home, I travel with Mum and Oli drives the car I came in. The sky this morning is utterly beautiful. Warm brushstrokes of pink and orange. Is this what the world looks like without him? When we get back to Mill Cottage, Mum goes straight to bed and falls asleep. Months of residual exhaustion take over – her mind has been a twenty-four-hour radio station of worry, questions, planning, washing, ironing, admin, food in Thermoses, pills, text messages, recorded voice WhatsApps. It gasps for a bit of air – peace.

I check on her regularly. She occasionally pokes her head out from under her nest of pillows, clothes and newspapers and blinks at me, rubbing her eyes, forehead folding in, saying, 'I can't believe it. I can't believe it's actually happened.' The sleeping and rewaking and not believing and sleeping goes on and on. The waking and the holding of the breath, mind foggy with fatigue, until all the fragments come together and the picture is clear again, burying back into the pillow with a long sigh and a sick feeling.

I go for a long walk with Boris. I do it because I feel that it's what Dad would have done. It feels like a final handhold. A connection to him, my feet treading the towpath that he loved. The dog that he loved. The towpath that has been my constant friend over the past few months. And which I've waded through, slick with mud, Boris covered and splattered to the waist.

Meanwhile, at home, Marcus has come, carrying a roast chicken wrapped in foil and a tea towel from some friends in the village. It was meant to be their lunch, but when they heard the news, they wanted to send it to us. It is so kind.

Marcus has been sitting with Oli for an hour and is just about to leave when I get back. We offer him another cup of tea, and he stays. We sit. We talk. We reminisce. We cry a little. He nods. Listens. Comfortable with the yawning silences, demonstrating to us that they are OK. We don't need to be polite and fill in cracks and gaps, which is a relief. He doesn't press us to. He just smiles, maintains eye contact, holding taut the thread of conversation as it naturally unwinds.

He has been sitting with us for another hour and is just about to leave when Mum gets up. We offer him another cup of tea, and again he stays.

That night I lie in bed wondering if Dad can see me, hear me. I feel certain that he can.

Funeral Arrangements
14 January 2013

Very quickly we have to make plans. We have a funeral to arrange. On 14 January, just two days later, we have three appointments in the diary. 10.30 a.m.: meeting with the funeral director. 1 p.m.: lunch with Uncle Tim, who is bringing food and funeral orders of service. We are all really looking forward to seeing him. And then at 4 p.m. we have scheduled a chat with Marcus about the service.

The funeral director is, on first meeting, quite a tall and imposing man, but he has a soft voice and the gentlest handshake I have ever encountered in my life. It is the handshake of a man who is fearful of touching anything too strongly, for fear of waking the dead. I spend a while wondering what his name would be if he was a character in a Dickens novel.

He sits down, and before we talk about anything, he says that he wants to just acknowledge that 'you've lost yer dad'. He looks briefly mournful and mentions his own mother, with whom he was clearly very close.

We talk about the different options available to us. He suggests the coffin that he'd chosen for 'Mum', which was of excellent quality but not ridiculously expensive. He asks us to give him a set of clothes for Dad to be buried in. The identifying item in this selection is his beautiful Balliol blazer, recently gifted to him by his female crew at Balliol College. There is also a pair of pink Leander Club socks, a pink tie and a blue-and-white-striped shirt that Mum always admired him in.

Next we have lunch with Tim, who is wearing a cashmere jumper, much like Dad often did, and is tall and generally enough like Dad to make me cry on him several times. It is comforting and reassuring to have him with us. We listen to music that we like, discuss hymns and potential readings. We agree that all of the children – Ol, Kate, Ed and I – will deliver the speech we wrote for Dad's seventieth. So often when someone dies, an incredible eulogy is written for them that they never hear. So we are comforted by the fact that Dad had heard our poem – and greatly enjoyed it.

By the end of the day, an email is sent out, setting the funeral date for 20 January. Just under a week's time.

> Dear friends,
>
> As you will have heard, Nick's funeral is private and for family only. However, so many people have been such good friends to him and us over the years, particularly in the past few difficult months, that we feel that so many have become an extension of our family.
>
> We would love you to join us at Nick's funeral on Monday 20 January at midday at St Mary's Church. Do join us afterwards at Mill Cottage for a glass or two of fizz to toast Nick.
>
> I'll be in touch again with logistics like where to park, etc., but I hope that's enough information at the moment.
>
> With all our love, Annabel, Kate, Ed, Oliver & Emily

We bicker about the order of service. But, overall, having a funeral to arrange is the kindest thing for a group of people who are newly grieving and don't know what to do with themselves. I get in a flap about fonts. Ed gets in a flap about formats. Oli flaps about the correct wording of hymns. We flap our way towards the funeral.

The Funeral Chapel
15 January 2013

Today we go into town to pick up the orders of service from the printer, and to visit Dad for the last time. The funeral home is a nondescript building tucked way behind a car park in the town centre. The reception area is reminiscent of the family room at the John Radcliffe. A soft handshake of a room.

I have a letter in my pocket that I've written to Dad and want him to be buried with. We wait patiently until someone comes to collect us and we are taken through to the funeral chapel. This is a small, candlelit room with a lectern and an open Bible at one end, with Dad's open coffin beneath. It is eerily cold. And there, in his funeral regalia, Dad is – or isn't. The clothes are his. It is definitely him, but it also isn't.

I think to myself, *Here I am with you, but you're not here at all. You're outside. You're bouncing on a branch in the car park. Blowing the leaves around on the tarmac.* The thought makes me smile. I have an image of Dad as a butterfly who has been released from a jar. Trapped in his body, a fleshy prison. He is now free, drawing noughts and crosses in the sky.

Homecoming
19 January 2014

The Night Before the Funeral
Last night the storm came.
Leaves. Twigs. Debris. Such Damage.
Heaven's ice cubes fell.

We decide that on the night before the funeral we want to bring Dad up to the church privately, just as a family. We are anxious about how we would cope seeing him carried in a coffin, and also like the idea of Dad being settled, having had a peaceful night before his burial. We arrange for the undertakers to bring the hearse to Mill Cottage first, for just a few moments' grace.

This is a very special and poignant time. A deep regret of ours is that Dad was never able to come back from hospital. To see Boris, to be surrounded by all his things, the familiar rooms and smells and dusty hemlines of his life. So it is very important to us that on 19 January, in the early evening, he finally comes home.

The sight of a hearse has always given me a little chill, and no more so than on my front drive, containing my own father. It is surreal to see it here, this huge, dark shadow of a car, and the row of almost Victorian-looking gentlemen in funeral regalia that empty out of it, standing formally, eyes low so as not to trespass on our privacy. Our faces are all pale, stricken.

When the time comes, the enormous hearse descends down the drive, and solemnly we follow, up the hill and through the village, passing some friends out on a walk, who take off their hats and lower their heads as a mark of respect. Outside the church, the Dickensian pallbearers expertly lift Dad out of the hearse, heave him up on to their shoulders and process into the church, led at the front by our kindly undertaker, who I can't help but notice is absolutely in his element, and truly seems to love his job.

The candles in the church have been lit, and Marcus is waiting for us at the door. I walk at the back, holding Boris tight on a lead. He is upset, whining, excited. The organist plays music as we come in, and as we say prayers, the dog settles. Privately we say goodbye.

The Funeral

20 January 2014

On the morning of Dad's funeral, I get an email from an online supermarket telling me that for a limited time if I buy Persil, I will get Comfort free. If only it were true.

Despite the extraordinary panic about where on earth people are going to park in our tiny village, the day is going well. I don't think Mum has ever looked more beautiful. It is as if a sense of calm has fallen on all of us, a reassuring hand resting on our shoulders. The church is jam-packed with our closest friends and family, and 'Dear Lord and Father of Mankind' rings out and echoes around the small stone space. Oli speaks brilliantly and movingly. We even manage to croak out Dad's seventieth speech, which goes down well. I hold it together until the last word, where my throat catches. Throughout the service, I am distracted by a butterfly that dances around the stained-glass window.

When we eventually bring Dad out to be buried, the clouds part and we are all warmed by the most incredible bright, dazzling sunshine. It feels like Dad has finally been granted his movie moment. Afterwards, we invite everyone home to Mill Cottage, where the furniture is pushed right back against the walls, allowing our home to be full of more love and people than it has ever contained before.

A Stone in My Shoe

21 January 2014

I am picked up at 5 a.m. to be driven back to Manchester to return to work. By some miracle, I have been able to stay home for all of this time and I am so grateful for this. I now need to get myself together and through these final weeks of filming.

Friends check in regularly and I tell them that I've gone from feeling tremendously heavy to totally normal, to hugely emotional, to just plain knackered. I think probably because it is such a huge thing – losing a parent – it takes a really long time to sink in. Almost like I'm standing in front of it and it's too massive to see the sides... I need distance and perspective.

My godmother Milly sends me an email:

> Butterflies. I have just looked up the significance after death.
> It is symbolic of the resurrection. Of a new birth, the start of a new spirit!!!!!!!!!
> It's the sign... look it up.
> Milly

True Grit
I limp a little, secretly.
A stone in my shoe.
A little piece of gravel
from the storm-ravaged drive
which I raked
in place of you.

In your old green coat
I recreated your sound
redistributed the drive
and made all even.
The rhythmic rattle
of metal on gravel.

Now three hours away by train,
a tiny piece of stone
invisible even to myself
pierces each step
and takes me home.

I feel like I'm experiencing the world differently: senses
heightened, eyes opened, drawn to the steadfastness of nature –
a sanctuary where Dad's spirit seems to diffuse into everything,
making it appear more beautiful. Every little bird a cheerful
messenger from beyond.

Spring. Hope
Waking from a winter dream
through the mossy, compost haze
I take in the washed-out world.
The cool, bleached colours.
The bruised body of earth
now firmer underfoot,
more confident.

A distant clattering of church bells chime
with an orchestra of chattering birds
and the stream seems to applaud
as it gushes
strong
after its frozen sleep.

It was you
when the sun broke through.
I feel your warmth like a guiding hand on my back
as I tread your path.
As I walk the same track.

The View from Seven Years On

The death of a parent topples your foundations, shifts the fault lines, throws you off balance and brings so many feelings, old and new, up to the surface. It takes time to regain your sense of place. Losing Dad has affected me in many curious and far-reaching ways. I'm still Emily, in full technicolour, but a little bit of grey has seeped into the palette. And the palette is always changing tone. Grief – in its newest, rawest form – was both adrenalising and utterly exhausting. A non-tangible, empty feeling that pervaded everything; a constant hum of anxiety under the surface, nervously filling the cracks in conversation. I struggled to be myself. I guess because 'myself' was inexorably changed . . . the new version still buffering. For a long time, I found it hard to laugh. Or cry. I could feel strangely detached and dry-eyed in one moment, and then quite suddenly be overwhelmed by the most intense and devastating tsunami of grief that would take my breath away and leave me dishevelled, mascara running down each surprised cheek. And then in the next moment I would feel fine again.

My main coping mechanism, apart from listening to recordings of his voice, and burying my face in his sweaters (oh the agony when one of them accidentally found its way into the wash), was keeping busy. Occupying my days and propelling myself at life as energetically as I could somehow kept me in balance. I was lucky therefore to escape into a number of acting roles which absorbed my restless energy and kept me distracted. Although it would be fair to say that death and grief followed me wherever I went. I have since played a grieving daughter, a grieving sister, a grieving wife and a grieving mother. I have committed suicide, had a terminal illness, been stabbed, strangled (and stuffed as a scarecrow) and have also snogged a serial killer.

I'd say it took me two years, a new relationship and an additional four months of backpacking together around India (with nothing to think about apart from what to eat and where to sleep) until I was properly ready to engage with it. To look at the ugly bits, feel the stinging regrets and relive the difficult chapters in an honest and painful way. Having wanted to run away, I felt a strong desire – a need, in fact – to pull down my notebooks and write them up, and in writing paragraph after paragraph, draft after draft, I felt like I was healing myself.

But I will never fully heal, and nor would I want to. The onion layers peel off to reveal fresh new hurts. In my fourth month of being pregnant, on a work trip to Rome, I went into a deserted chapel to light a candle for Dad, and wept with the realisation that he would never meet my baby. That he would never do 'this is the way the lady rides' or 'squeeze relax' or make mazes for her in the sand. Now that Romy is here I frequently burst into tears trying to explain to her that Grandpa Nick on the fridge is 'Mummy's daddy'. He would have loved her so much. And she him. I don't really allow myself to dwell on these thoughts too often as I fear I could trip and fall down a veritable landslide of feeling. My heart still reaches for him, as Romy reaches her arms for me. The aching loss is just a thought away.

But something that comforts me is the idea that in losing Dad in life, I gained someone on my team upstairs, pulling strings: a guiding hand. As I was nervously walking to the read-through of *Doc Martin* in early 2015, at a riverside location in Hammersmith, I was practically knocked over by a boat that came out of the water just in front of me onto the towpath. The name on the side? Nick Bevan. When I first met my husband Billy, there were so many strange coincidences around our coming together that I felt almost certain that Dad had played a part in arranging it. Maybe this is just my way of dealing with the disappointment that the two were never able to meet. Or maybe it was fate, *kismet*? Maybe it doesn't matter, if it helps, even just a bit, to try and find meaning where there is none. I do continue to feel that Dad is close, keeping a watchful eye over me (although he could perhaps up his game a bit in the parking-ticket department). Likewise, Mum, seven years on, still feels that Dad is in her life. She is grateful and surprised that she still feels his presence so strongly, and the fulfilment and comfort that that brings. The memories are fresh. Right there. She can transport herself to the left-hand side of his hospital bed, where she is breaking into tears, and Dad is catching her eye, saying, 'Don't worry about me, I can cope.'

I recently attended the funeral of a dear friend's father, and as I turned to see his coffin making its entrance into the chapel, a muscle memory crept into my body. A contraction at the back of the throat, a stinging of the eyes and a pressing of my tongue into bottom teeth. Death casts a long shadow. I looked at my friend and I saw that her eyes were full of disbelief. She had planned every detail of this perfect farewell, yet she was still in shock as she watched it unfold. I saw her pain and I knew it. But it was also hers, and hers only, defined by the unique quality of her relationship with her father, a rich tapestry woven over their thirty-eight years. When the curtain opened to take her father away, it held his coffin in a billowing embrace, the fabric lifting and falling. I couldn't help imagining his final breaths. I wished that there was a way to take her pain away. But I know that loving someone comes at a cost. It will hurt. I wish it didn't, but it will, and she has to feel it, wade through it, a day at a time, being kind and gentle to herself, until she regains her footing and feels lighter again.

I hope that the love they shared will sustain her and that, one day, the memories of her father at the very end will soften, and the happier memories will start to break through the surface like new buds.

Endnotes

It is amazing how grief can bond you with people. And fast. Despite the fact that all of our circumstances are different, there is a shorthand that exists. As a way of drawing this book to a close, I wanted to open out the lens and share the unique voices of friends of mine who are also processing the loss of a parent – or in some cases, both parents. I have arranged these entries in time order, dating from the most recent.

Anna. One year

On Wednesday, it was a year since I last saw you, since we spent the day together, but I didn't really chat to you because I was throwing salad ingredients onto plates and nagging you for not baking enough potatoes. It was a day of hosting close family and friends – Bella's baptism – with that air of taut conviviality those days bring. The Boat Race was on in the background. We took the kids outside to hunt for Easter eggs. You'd been to the library and borrowed books to keep them all entertained. I wish I'd stopped to thank you.

I kissed you goodbye and gave you a hug. I still strain to remember any details of it – was it warm and enthusiastic? Did we, as sometimes happened, bash sunglasses or cheekbones or stand on each other's feet?

My last view of you was in my wing mirror as we pulled away, waving your big goodbye wave in the warm evening sunshine – a day much like today – with Mum waving next to you.

And that was it.

Goodbye.

Three days later, you died of a cardiac arrhythmia in your sleep. You were sixty-five.

My dad died… since Dad died… when Dad died… the words still stick in my throat. A year on, I can still be torn apart by a motorway sign or your favourite marzipan chocolate bar in the newsagent. But looking back to my writing from this time last year, I realise I have crawled some distance from the wreckage. I have crawled through agony, fear, rage, hopelessness, apathy and longing to a sadness and pain that still sting my eyes but no longer take the breath from my lungs.

People say, 'You must be glad to see the back of this year.' Yes, it has been comfortably the most terrible year of my life, but it's also a year that connects me to Dad, that he was part of, and a year that gives me permission to grieve and be sad. In the lead-up to this anniversary, my mind has been lurching around, searching for a direction of travel, a position, a status quo, but my emotional compass is broken, and I'm lost.

I have found grief so disorientating, so disorderly. I had some notion that it would be a solid thing that I could place in a box in my head marked 'Sad Stuff' (maybe even 'Extremely Sad Stuff'?) and keep it there. Big and painful but neatly contained, somehow. But it hasn't been solid or neat. It has seeped into every corner of my being over this past year, rattled every bone. It has changed my character. It has made me impatient with my children, irritable with my husband, withdrawn and anxious, lacking in confidence at work and with friends, restless yet apathetic, angry but timid, battling so hard yet barely breaking even.

Like most grieving humans, I have searched out those little life rafts in the shipwreck: wine, running (slowly), *Fawlty Towers* (the only TV I could watch for weeks). I have slowed the tempo of my life to walking pace, and taken time to write, listen to and read a lot about other people's experiences of grief: Julia Samuel's *Grief Works*, C. S. Lewis's *A Grief Observed*, Cariad Lloyd's *Griefcast* podcast series, a load of accounts on Instagram (@lifedeathwhat, @thegriefcase, @sketchesfromthecave) and the wonderful *Signs: The Secret Language of the Universe* by Laura Lynne Jackson.

Now, a year on, when I'm having a good day, I feel like I might be starting to stitch together a new relationship with Dad, a patchwork of memories, conversation patterns that I can tap out to myself, and new signs, those 'meaningful coincidences' that strengthen my belief that he's around us, wringing his hands and trying his best to hold us steady. It's not the version of him I wanted – that's the one with the big wave and not enough baked potatoes – but in the absence of that model, it's the version I've got to live with.

Alex. One year

My father died from Covid and just typing those words takes my breath away. Almost a year on and every day brings fresh torment from this vile pandemic that has gripped the world and eats away at every headline. My father was an exceptional man.

Most people think that about their father, but every day I am reminded of how lucky I was to have him for thirty-eight years; if only it could have be thirty-eight more.

My journey through grief is ongoing and in many ways surprising. When the sheer shock of it unfolded, I wanted to submerge myself under the duvet covers and close the curtains for a year, which may sound wonderfully gothic, but the reality required me to be far more practical. When you lose a parent while being a parent, you realise you simply have to keep going. The kids needed stability and they needed a mother who was present for them and it was as simple as that.

Dreaded home-schooling started two days after we buried Dad, and my grief had to be corralled and packaged into rare, snatched moments when it could expose itself, usually when the children were occupied or tucked up in bed. It would emerge as I would stow the laundry, fresh tears streaking the white sheets or trickling down my cheeks while doing the washing-up with my back turned to the usual chaos of the kids' suppertime. When schools finally reopened their doors and the kids went back, my grief exploded, finally given room to rage, and I became proficient at driving home with sobs coursing through my body.

In some ways I have found that my grief is surprisingly solitary. I am lucky enough to have an incredible husband, family and friends, but my grief is a journey I navigate alone. My mother, lost adrift in her grief, lives a five-hour drive away, so while we are sharing a similar voyage, it has felt like our life rafts are miles apart.

Modern technology is a Pandora's box when someone dies. My father's number tops my iPhone 'favourites' list and while I feel a heart-searing pain when I glimpse it, I still don't want to delete it from my life. At almost a year on I am still not strong enough to retrace the steps to our last text conversations, and the mere thought of recalling our farewell over FaceTime brings hot tears to my eyes. Yes, time heals, but it takes me further from our last touch, conversation and hug.

Small shards of light do appear. We may not have his physical being, but I take great comfort from hearing his voice and seeing his presence in the everyday and keeping who he was alive in my memory. His face now beams at me from various photos around the house and I find myself heeding his advice and filling up bird feeders or turning off needless lights; all remnants of Dad shining through in my day-to-day life.

Night-time sometimes holds its rare delights and on the odd, exquisite occasion I come across Dad in my dreams, I awake clinging to every vivid detail, craving for more. Childlike as it seems, I often daydream about what I would do and say if he could be brought back to Earth for just five minutes. Instead I have to seek solace in tracing the hands of his trusty old watch or inhaling his much-loved green cashmere jumper that now resides uncomfortably in my wardrobe.

My biggest fear is that I will lose those intricate and precious details that make up my memories of him – the way he would clear his throat, the twinkle in his eye and his stance among a crowd – knowing that they will fade with the tides of time. For now, I look for Dad in birdsong and in nature, and seek comfort from trying to live my life how he believed life should be lived. With laughter, love and kindness.

Priya. One year

I feel so blessed. My father and I shared an incredibly close and special bond. Deeply, passionately loving... it was an intensely charged relationship that could be quite combustible! But by God, I loved that man and he loved me with such complete devotion, and I miss the power of his love so much. Its presence in the world inside me enriches me and, when I long for him, its absence gnaws at my heart. He is an absent presence, a present absence. And learning to live without him has been just that – like learning a whole new way of being and, to some extent, a whole new identity as a daughter without a father.

As I write, I can still feel, smell, visualise, hear, sense my beloved pa all around me. I love and cherish the vividness and sense of him that I carry all the time. He is everywhere. And nowhere. It is agony confronting that reality, and as the first anniversary of his death approaches, I worry that the sharpness of my memories will fade. In the final trimester of my first pregnancy last August, my beloved pa died. It was not unexpected, but no less devastating to lose him. I was with him when he died with us at home and the atmosphere around him was infused with much sorrow, beauty and love. I treasure that memory, and in all honesty, the moment of his death was not nearly as ghastly as I had feared it might be.

I have been fortunate to actively care for my parents over the years, so our level of involvement in each other's day-to-day lives has been significant. In some ways, I think this has made his absence more palpable, as I live in a physical environment so full of memories of him. My parents both had international careers, so we spent a lot of my childhood apart. This made living in close proximity, when they retired to the UK ten years ago, hugely appealing, and I am so glad that we had this experience. Our love as a family has always been infused with longing, only now the longing has a different feel because the longed-for reunions of childhood can never be realised in the present or future. But we really did squeeze every last drop out of life over the last decade that my father was ill; we lived in 'extra time' as he defied his bleak prognosis, and consequently were so blessed to say and do so much together over the years, both important and trivial.

As Auden understood so well, it feels utterly wrong that time marches forth when we lose a beloved. I have often asked myself over this last year, how do I somehow find the energy, the strength, the hope to step into each day when my broken, grieving heart is weighing me down so heavily? And yet, somehow, the momentum of life carries us forward. Life has its own rhythm and its own plans.

I get floored by grief from time to time, but for the most part, I speak of Dad when he comes into my mind and weep when I need to, and I write. A lot. It feels so strange to speak of him in the past tense. There are moments that really catch me out: when, say, the other day, I put my hand in his favourite jacket that I remember him wearing on our last day out last summer and I find a jingle of coins and a handful of the sweets he loved, and always had with him. I held those sweets and coins in my hands for several minutes, marvelling at the thought that his were the last human hands to touch these and now those hands that I was so used to holding and massaging and stroking have gone. For ever.

But saying that, I find it fascinating how we imbue so many things with meaning when we lose our loves. Scattering Dad's ashes in the places I walk each day was so perfect, and I love the thought that he is now in the trees and creatures around me. I gaze at and talk to them often, as if communing with him. Today I walked past a common where some of his ashes were sprinkled, among a spray of daffodils dancing in the late-spring sunshine. Today, in high summer, people are back to playing cricket on that common and I love the thought of Dad 'watching' them. He loved both playing and watching that gentle game.

Yes, my grief for my father assumed greater proportions after our girl arrived, his absence feeling more palpable, but a truly wonderful discovery was that I felt closer to him than ever in discovering the power and intensity of my love as a parent. Although it is still relatively early days for me in this new landscape of loss, I am interested in how the experience of pain has changed. In the earliest months, the waves of grief were like body blows and I sometimes had to hold on to something solid to steady myself as my body convulsed with tears. Now the pain is less like an earthquake of grief tearing through me, and more like a tide that comes in regularly, lapping at my soul, but not threatening to drown me.

As I write, my mother is dying, ravaged by a rare and vicious degenerative neurological disorder. I contrast the now quite gentle gnawing sadness of my grief for Dad with the devastating mourning that has become part of my reality as I bear anguished witness to her living losses, as every meaningful capacity ebbs away from her. I dread the tsunami of grief that will come when she dies, but I also know that it is simply a part of an ocean of grief that I shall grow used to living with.

Natasha. Ten years

They say that the pain of losing someone gets easier with time. In my experience, I can confirm that this is true. The anniversaries hurt less and the sudden memories that pop up don't seem to hit like bullets any more. More like getting hit by someone's bag on the Tube; it knocks you, but it's tolerable. But as I approach the eleventh year of losing my mum, I have found a new fear creeping in. The fear of forgetting. As the years pass by, I move further and further away from that last conversation, that last touch. I worry about forgetting what she looked and sounded like. How she made me feel. Sometimes, when I close my eyes, I worry that I don't see her as clearly any more.

I found out recently that each time you replay memories, details change; you forget things, you mix them up, you never fully replay the memory exactly as it was. This I find hard to swallow, because memories are all you have to hold on to.

Sometimes I try to replay whole scenes from the really painful times, but it's like my body/mind has blocked them out. Recorded over them like a VHS. There are years missing where I've no idea what really happened, I just know it was hard. But I need the good memories to find comfort. To know that it was real. So my remedy for this? The senses. I keep a little bottle of her perfume in the drawer by my bed. One sniff and I am instantly transported. The memories suddenly become so strong. When I need to feel her around me, I play her favourite Northern soul music, which immediately fills me with her spirit. And where looking at photos used to feel almost too painful, my eyes now welcome the memories that float in on glancing at her face. I welcome them with open arms like I would her. She is always around me; we are one and the same. But sometimes we just need to open up our other receptors to know that the people we have lost are close. There are still times in life where my body suddenly feels eight years old, and the little girl longs for her mother. I thought that would go away with age, but I reckon even when I'm eighty I'll have that longing. I still get that strange feeling whenever I meet someone new, or I'm doing a job. At some point people ask about my parents. Where are they from? Do you go home often? Is your mum or dad black? I get that weird embarrassment feeling, and I play out the sentence in my head. Should I say my mum's *from* Wigan, or *was* from Wigan? Do I say my mum's *dead*, or, 'I don't *have* my mum any more'? It feels cringy. Not just for me. But also for the person asking. You see they feel awkward. Always. A quick change of subject to a Netflix documentary or a starling they saw three days ago tends to help diffuse the situation. People are awkward about death. Especially British people. Even though we lose people all the time.

It's completely unavoidable. But it still hurts like hell.

Mike. Twenty-one/fourteen years

I can't imagine what you're going through. Tears will visit you on their own terms. Time heals a bit, but don't put that pressure on yourself. You'll never forget. I'll never forget. You are not alone. I will never tire of talking to you about this.

Those would have been the perfect words for me to hear aged sixteen, when Mum (fifty-five) died of cancer, and again, seven years later, when Dad (sixty-two) died of the same.

Dear Mum. If she was known for being difficult to get close to, I was closest. My last memory is of giving her daffodils in hospital, picked from a roadside bank near to where I now live. 'Yes, yellow,' through morphine's eyes. And of Dad: a final beaming wave through his window in Tasmania, where he had come to spend half of each year. We knew it was the last time. Forever my hero, we enjoyed a sublime father–son relationship. Take-off. The plane's ascent tracks down the river near his house. I think I can see... The clouds come. Abyss.

'Grief', the price we pay for love, is as common to the human condition as it is personal. Just as 'birth' claims its label, and yet is necessarily unique.

My grief odyssey has taught me much, little of which I could have stowed at the outset. I have taped my personal chart together under passage, mostly with cuttings from books. Professional help has eluded me. Perhaps it can still help me.

One book needs special mention: Victor Frankl's *Man's Search for Meaning*. As a survivor of Holocaust concentration camps, he presents vital thinking from the point of view of total suffering. 'Everything can be taken from a man but one thing: the last of the human freedoms – to choose one's attitude in any given set of circumstances, to choose one's own way.' This finally made sense of the awkward stoic reflex I unconsciously bestowed on myself at the onset of grief. I was exercising something I could still control when all else was lost.

What kept hauling me out of bed in the morning was an idea. I will rebuild what I have lost; I will find my way back to a home and a family. This became my private obsession, a vision in technicolour, while life often seemed grey. Frankl states, 'Those who have a "why" to live, can bear with almost any "how".' This has been my 'why'.

Taking both wisdoms together enabled me to get my arms around my grief. I decide how this story ends.

*

Of course, the idea needed another actor. Alexandra and I have been together for eighteen years. My idea became our idea. She is the dazzling axis around which our three beautiful children and I now orbit. But with our idea hanging in spectacular reality, I've noticed my grief reinventing itself. I wish they could know us. I hope they're proud.

And, in its cruellest twist, a question: 'My, haven't you grown?' I work harder, love better, look deeper, feel stronger. This is not to pose proficiency, only improvement through coping with the loss of my parents. What of my 'now' would I give for my 'then'? And what of the odyssey? To unwind it all would be a cosmic collapse back to a Mike I have sailed too far from, that I wouldn't recognise. But I'd have my parents back. Therein lies my unwritten book.

Thank heavens for memories: irrevocable permanence with that maturing quality, absent the present's tension and the future's uncertainty. Along time's continuum, do they all simply co-exist? Frankl reassures, 'Instead of possibilities, I have realities in my past, not only the reality of work done and love loved, but of sufferings bravely suffered. These sufferings are even the things of which I am most proud, though these things are things that cannot inspire envy.'

Sara. Twenty-two/twenty-one years
How to prepare for our parents' deaths?
Mine were separated by fifteen months.
She, March 15th 1997. He, June 15th 1998.

Hers, where she'd dreaded, in hospital.

Alone.

That, my greatest regret.

Although seriously ill, her death inevitable, there was nothing to indicate on Friday afternoon that she would be gone by 8 a.m. on Saturday, and so we weren't with her. It had been hard for her in hospital. For my father too. And for me. She was eighty-seven, sweet and so brave.

I had to be practical and strong – for my mother while she still lived, for my father losing his wife and rock after she died. We struggled a bit together in our grief and loss. Different dynamics. Edgy.

Prickly.

His death, unexpected on a favourite walk. An aortic embolism. He was ninety-two. Collapse in the street. Some hours before I found out. Shock. Again, needing to be practical. Harrowing journey following ambulance in my car as we changed hospitals. I was alone. Made the wrong choice – or did I? – in not staying at the hospital. I knew it was serious but, in shock, got confused. Exhausted. Went home. That call from the hospital the next morning: 'Your father is poorly.' It means dying.

A Tube strike, intense road traffic. I missed his end by twenty minutes. But I did for him what I failed to do for my mother and what she would have wanted me to do for him – I helped the male nurse wash and clean and cherish my father's body before gently zipping up the bag. Once a shroud. It was easy, natural.

The funeral arrangements for my parents were different. Both cremated at Golders Green, where we'd attended countless funerals over countless years. Hers delayed, time to plan. I took precious little things to put in her simple coffin. A letter, a tiny little teddy bear, some glittering red hearts to be sprinkled over her. My father disapproved.

My huge regret that I didn't ask where she would be taken after her death on the ward. Where did they take her? That haunts me still. My father was Jewish – the cremation arranged quickly; also I was at the National Theatre and going to the USA with Michael Frayn's play *Copenhagen*.

He died on Monday. We cremated him on Friday. I flew out on Saturday. He wasn't a practising Jew, but someone asked if I'd be saying Kaddish. I hadn't planned to. Later I wondered if I'd made a mistake. So on the anniversary of his death a dear friend came with me to the tiny synagogue in Princelet Street, close to my father's East End roots, and Kaddish was said.

Their ashes are mingled beneath an ancient olive tree in the South of France on land belonging to lifetime friends. It is a comfort to know they are together. The ashes different colours – yin and yang! Hers paler than his. I wonder why? They were remarkable people. I miss them. Hugely. They cherished and encouraged but never spoilt their only child.

Each day, applying makeup in my bedroom, I see reflected in the mirror her photo behind me – looking over my shoulder, as it were. Looking back to my own image, I now look like her twin.

Lipstick
On the day my mother died
I slipped my arms
into her cardigan –

black wool mixed with silk
her favourite,
on her small frame serving as a coat –
and on my lips
the lipstick from her bag
until the summer robs me
of the extra layer
and the lipstick is no more.

Rory. Thirty-three years

I was little when Dad died, so there's no doubt it intrinsically formed who I am and how I see the world. I knew he loved me, though, that he wouldn't have wanted my life to be ruined by his death and that my happiness gave him pleasure. So I deliberately chose to take the positives from the experience, to grant him my happiness, and to protect it, in his memory. To not give into the rage or the feelings of futility and unfairness, but to allow that young trauma to crystallise for me the genuine and the important. It wasn't always easy, obviously, and the intensity of adolescent feeling certainly wobbled my resolve now and again. I don't mean I suppressed any negative feelings – I would readily give in to crying if I felt I needed to. Crying is the only balm we have. But I would always come back to the fact that I knew he would have done whatever he could to protect and nourish my comfort, learning and joy. Just because he had a stupid accident and didn't come home one day didn't fundamentally change that. And so I tried to make sure that I looked out for those things for myself, for him. It was, and continues to be, a way of paying tribute to his life. Because it does continue. I still cry about it, about him, thirty-three years later.

Sometimes it's because I feel sorry for that little boy having to deal with such vastness of experience at such a young age, particularly when I see the carefree spirits of my own children at a similar age. Sometimes I feel sorry for my mum, of the weight of care she was forced to undertake while severed from her own source of comfort, learning and joy. And then there are the phantom losses that haunt me, the tears brought about as I mentally prepare myself for the deaths of those I love the most now, the subconscious attempt to steel myself against future pain, as if you can prepare for such a thing... But mainly it's because I feel sorry for him. Of what he didn't see. Of what he missed. Of course his spirit lives on; in us, in those who loved him. But I want his body to have reverberated with the love of his children as adults, his grandchildren, his remarkable wife, his creaking friends. I don't just want him to be talked about. I want him to be held.

That physical loss is the most potent. It's the most awful bit of a funeral. Because where, now the physical has fully gone, does the love for that person go? We learn, over years, that it goes to lots of places, and pops up at the most surprising of times. And while it feels unnatural at first to internalise a love that was physical, tactile and reciprocated, to turn it back on ourselves, it actually offers us a continued relationship with that person going forward. Why I don't necessarily feel sorry for myself, the me that is now, is that I continue to have an intensely personal relationship with my dad. And in death I don't have to share him with anybody. His death presence is mine alone; in life I knew he belonged to lots of people. I don't necessarily talk to him, except in occasional, much-cherished dreams. But he absolutely informs my decision-making, my work, my parenting, my aspirations, my sense of self, my perspective, my sense of humour. He's not the only person in my life that does that. But it illustrates how his premature death was an event, albeit an important one, in an otherwise unbroken and continuous umbrella of loving and considered parenting that he continues to offer me today.

Jason. Thirty-five years

When I was fourteen, when he was forty-three, my dad died of metastatic oesophageal cancer that had spread to his liver. He died two weeks after the liver cancer was discovered, a year after undergoing surgery and aggressive chemotherapy. My last or more recent memories of his life as I experienced it amount to three.

One. My grandfather carried his son carefully down the stairs at some point during those first two weeks of September. My 5'11" dad's familiar 200 lb weight had dropped to not much more than half that amount. I can recall the angle from downstairs where I watched.

Two. I remember the bustle as he was having trouble breathing with the oxygen set up at our house. A decision had been made to transport him from our suburban house to the University of Pennsylvania Hospital. I recall standing in the yard as the EMTs lifted the wheelchair high into the air, holding him up as on a royal palanquin, to quickly navigate the shortest line from door to ambulance across the maze of heaped flower beds and intricate landscaping.

Every year, including earlier that one, my dad and I spent spring weekends drawing up plans for the garden, filling the car with six-packs of seedlings, planting a quilting riot of living colour: marigolds, periwinkle, begonias, impatiens. My younger brother and my dad shared a passion for playing and watching seasonal sports year-round. That was their thing. Rather than sports, one of the things my dad instead shared with me was our love of nature, of joyfully going over the top planning and implementing our complex botanical blueprints for the yard. Neither my dad nor I could ever be considered morning people, and the two of us – through that year – would get the spades with blue rubber handles from the shed to dig down dens into the loamy mounds of soil and carefully loosen the roots of the annuals we had selected at the garden centre and place them carefully into the earth. We would continue long after dark, digging, feeling for rocks and roots in the way, mulching, surrounded by the odour of earth. The neighbours affectionately called us the night gardeners. By early September, the garden was in full splendour.

And now three. A few hours before he left that last time for the hospital, I walked past the door of his bedroom and saw him alone sitting on the edge of his bed – head down. He called my name, and I said I was busy, terrified of this dad I didn't recognise, hurrying on past into my room. My failure in that moment of courage and empathy, that lost chance to talk, is ever a searing regret, a stabbing fragment of coal that burns my heart. He would, that night, die alone in the hospital around 4 a.m. – when he left the house there had been no expectation that such was a possibility that night. I regret what I said just before he left, as he was, refusing the ambulance, sitting in the passenger side of the car, waiting to leave. I said through the rolled-down window, 'Be strong.' Those were my last words to him. I could have said instead, a thousand times, 'I love you.'

I think most of what I write and have written since then is an attempt to go back and revise those dumb young words.

My dad loved my art-making and creativity; my dad, proud of me, admitted defeat if we were arguing about a fact and it turned out I was right; my dad took us on weekends on mystery car rides to incredible secret places; my dad was a real-estate lawyer who took us camping and canoeing deep in the woods; my dad was the charismatic fun and goofing around that anchored my family. When I told him that I didn't want to play Little League and was hysterically crying in shame, he, former college star football player, scooped me up into his lap and hugged me and told me with a warm smile that he couldn't care less, wiped away my tears, and made absolutely clear to me that he thought I was amazing and how much he admired me just as I was. At his funeral, a man I had never seen before, a low-level clerk at the county courthouse, came up to me in tears to introduce himself and tell me what a good man my dad was; how my dad would always be sure to have a beer with him once a week; how supportive my dad had been during hard times. Weeks later, after the funeral, deep down in a pad of desktop-size paper on my desk, I found my dad's note for me, circled and underlined: 'You are the best.'

I wish my dad was here. I know how close we would be, all the adventures, by canoe, across mountains, long conversations, so many 'I love you's written, texted, spoken. Dad nurtured and encouraged my imagination, gave me permission to become my odd queer unique me, and, in so doing, also gave me the ability to robustly, creatively, imagine him here now. I miss him terribly. My mom was so deeply in love with him; his loss broke her heart in a way I can only begin to comprehend now, unimaginable to me then – and yet she tenaciously and with grace held and supported my brother and me, and does still. Every spring my mom, my nephews, my brother, me – we all surround his gravestone, digging, planting for him a many-textured colour explosion, a growing exuberance of hardy flowers.

Epilogue (I had a prologue, so…)

Halfway through writing *The Diary of Losing Dad*, and struggling somewhat, I opened up one of Dad's reference books called *Short Prayers for the Long Day*. I was looking for a passage that Dad had picked out for me when I lost my dear school friend Josie to breast cancer.

The passage he had picked out was by Oscar Wilde:

> 'Angrily spake the gardener, Who plucked this flower?
> One of the rarest in all my garden. Gently answered
> the Master. So dearly did I love it, I chose it for
> my own.'

I felt like I wasn't old enough or mature enough or worldly enough to be facing up to such huge feelings of loss, and at the time Dad took Mum and me up to our local church, where we linked arms and he read a number of passages to me that he felt would be of comfort. I remember not necessarily taking in the words but feeling hugely supported in my grief.

While looking through that particular book of his, I found another passage of poetry next to which Dad had written, 'For Em'. The discovery of my name, in his handwriting, felt almost electric. A connection. I couldn't help but feel that Dad was somehow speaking to me and giving me the guidance that I needed. The courage to go on with what I was trying to write.

The passage read:

> Hold on in the darkness, though no gleam of light breaks through.
> Keep on dreaming dreams although they never quite come true.
> Keep on moving forward though you don't know what's ahead.
> Keep on keeping on though it's a lonely road ahead.
>
> Keep on looking up towards the goal you have in view.
> Keep on at the task God has given you to do.
> Keep on in the hope that there are better times in store.
> Keep on praying for the thing that you are waiting for.

It was precisely the encouraging fatherly advice that I needed. One of Nick Bevan's famous motivational speeches, delivered at a crucial juncture. It felt like I had him back for one precious moment, and then lost him all over again.

Acknowledgements

As I'm an actor, you'll have to forgive me for treating this bit of the book like a sort of Oscar acceptance speech. I'D LIKE TO THANK MY MUM. But, I really would, because I have so much to thank her for. Mum, your support and love have always been boundless. Thank you for lemon chicken and Vinho Verde in times of hardship. Thank you for always, always being there. You wanted us to have the best opportunities in life, and encouraged us to pursue our dreams no matter what. For that I am eternally grateful. I'm sorry for using the f-word in the book and that it never worked out on the violin . . .

Billy, thank you for being my cheerleader. For encouraging me to write authentically and truthfully and for patiently listening as I tried to find the right words. I know it was like a slow form of torture for you. ('It sounds good Em, why are you changing it!') I'm grateful that you didn't allow me to rewrite the entire thing an hour before my deadline. Thank you for buying me oat lattes and surprise treats from the cafe when I'm feeling flat. Thank you for never tiring of talking about Dad. You've been a rainbow in my cloud. I love you.

Romy, I hope that you will read this one day and get to know that Grandpa Nick isn't just a face in photo albums. You are already the cleverest, funniest, most interesting person we know, and you bring us untold joy.

Thank you to Sarah Camlett for being a mentor and champion and for always encouraging me to write, in whatever form. And to Dan Copeland and Erin King too. Camlett corner has truly seen me at my best and worst, but never fails to make me laugh or lift my confidence.

Uncle Rich, Tiki Kyte, Anna Jones, Gabby Best, Helen Mumby, Laura Kaye – you all read early drafts of this, and your detailed and thoughtful advice meant the world to me.

Tash, Mike, Priya, Anna, Rory, Jason, Sara, Alex – thank you for bravely and generously agreeing to share your reflections on grief with me. They have added so much to the book and it is a privilege to share these pages with you. Jason (Zuzga!) – thank you also for inviting me to write for *Fence*, and for coaxing out all the extra material that was waiting in the wings.

To my siblings, Kate, Ed and Ol, I love you all and I hope you feel that I've done Dad justice. Ol – thanks for your pitch-perfect gag about hospital catering, which you came up with irritatingly quickly.

Peter Kyte, my father-in-law, thank you for your genius brainwave that helped me get over the finish line. I dearly hope the grammar was up to scratch. Miles Morland – thank you for being the genius brainwave. Roll on Quo Vadis.

Creating this book with Unbound has been such a rewarding process. Thank you, Joelle Owusu for commissioning the project! I'll never forget our first meeting. Martha Sprackland, I so appreciated getting your brilliant input on the poetry. Imogen, I couldn't have asked for a more responsive, supportive editor. A thousand thanks. Thanks also to Mark Ecob for the beautiful cover design and Anna Galbraith for publicity.

To all our family and friends – we couldn't have got through it without you. Likewise the amazing staff at the John Radcliffe and Witney Community Hospitals whose warmth, kindness and commitment never failed to move us.

Thank you to everyone whose name is listed in the back pages. Each one of you has made this book a reality and I hope I have done you all proud.

Unbound is the world's first crowdfunding publisher, established in 2011.

We believe that wonderful things can happen when you clear a path for people who share a passion. That's why we've built a platform that brings together readers and authors to crowdfund books they believe in – and give fresh ideas that don't fit the traditional mould the chance they deserve.

This book is in your hands because readers made it possible. Everyone who pledged their support is listed below. Join them by visiting unbound.com and supporting a book today.

A deeply appreciative Old
   Salopian
Farida Adot
Sapana Agrawal
Henry Andreae
Gurli Andreassen
Alyssa Arbuckle
Mark Arnell
Laurence Ash
Tory Ashby
Tressa Ballard
Sian Barnes
Mike Bayley
Oliver Bayliss
Val Bayliss-Brideaux

Richard Beacroft
Jane Beaufoy
Tim Beaumont
Debbie Beharrell
Sabine Bein
Gemma Benbow
Annabel Bevan
Ed Bevan
Oliver Bevan
Richard Bevan
Tim and Penny Bevan
Sophie Binyon
Mary Birdsong
Gemma Bond
Kildare Bourke-Borrowes

Sarah Bourke-Borrowes

Thea Bourke-Borrowes

Susan Bovell

Zoe Boyle

Brazen Productions

Rachel Bruce

Verity Bruce

Katherine Bryan

Amy Buik

Alison Bunn

Lesley Burvill-Holmes

Angie Butler

Mary Butler

Briana Camacho

Sarah Camlett

Jonny Campbell

Tim Cashmore

Zeira Castillon

Kevin Castle

Nicholas Cave

Mark Chavez

Tim Chipping

Ed Christian

Tim Clifford Hill

Will Cohen

Pandora Colin

Ben Collier-Marsh

Christopher and Caroline
    Compston

Rhys Connolly

Katie Constable

Lowri Cook

Sarah Cook

Katharine Cooper

Dan Copeland

Mizuno Corporations

Anna Corrie

Matthew Corrie

Natasha Cottriall

Jake Courage

Jill Crawford

Lisa Cunningham

Sarah Davey-Hull

Andrew de Perlaky

Stuart de Turberville

Diana Deverell

Melissa Digby-Bell

Bertie Dixon

Poppy Dixon

Charlotte Dolman

Alistair Donegan

Jack Dow

Allison Drennan

Ruth Easby

Ed Eccles

Barry Edwards

Anton Egorov

Humphrey Elles-Hill

Boglarka Erdei

Daniel Evaristi Boyd

F A Albin & Sons

Beniamin Fabiński

Bush family

Graeme Feggetter

Milly Fink

Debbie Forbes

Celine Fortier

Randy Fortunato

Chris Fortune

Fiona Fountain

Claire Fourel

Michael Fox

Jamie Fraser

Tors Fraser

John Frewin

Josh Gaillemin

Susan Gardiner

Henry Garrett

Matt Garrill

Rebecca Gatward

Dacey Geary

Hana Gee

Anja Georgi

Rachel Gibson

Karan Gill

Leah Good

Alice Gordon

Poppy Gordon Lennox

Sophie & Richard Goulding

Miriam Goy

Nick Gray

Sarah Green

Trudi Groom

Jane Guernier

Annemari Hallanoro

Michael Hamilton

Sam Handbury-Madin

Amy Hanson

Alice Harrison

Paul Harrop

Tom Hawksfield

Andrew Hawley

James and Elly Hayward

Jane Healy

Dudley Heesom

Giulietta Hextall

Priscilla Higham

Ali Hines

Natasha Hobday

Rebecca Hodgson

Ximena Holliday

Sophie Holt

Charlotte Hopkinson

Tom Hoskyns

Katharine Iliffe

David Isherwood

Fiona James

Jacquie Jenner

Graham Johnson

Zoe Johnson

Gail Jones

Nick Jones

Laura Kaye

Hanghang Ke

Gwendolyn Keasberry

Jay Kelly

Izzy Kemp

Ruth Kenley-Letts

Sara Kestelman

Anna Kibbey

James Kibbey

Cassia Kidron

Dan Kieran

Mi-Yeon Kim

Birgit Klobert

Suzanne Korff

Atlanta Kyte

Billy Kyte

Peter Kyte

Tiki Kyte

Dominic Labram

Sam Laurie

Bryony Lavery

Hannah Lee

David and Norma Levin

Anna Lewis

James Lewis

Catherine Lightbody

Nikki Livingstone-Rothwell

Carlos Lloyd

John Lloyd

Charles Lowndes

Hugo Lowry

Nic Lowry

Kate Luxton

Rory Macewen

Zoë MacLachlan

Louisa Macmillan

Emmy Maddy Johnston

Priya & Will Man

Lucy Marshall

Jack Matthews

Ben McMillan

Andrew Miles

John Mitchinson

Dee Montague

Deborah Morgan

Miles Morland

Richard Anthony Morris

Emilie Morse

Helen Mortimer

Robin Mounsey

Robin Mulvihill

Carlo Navato

Alex Nesbit

Luke Newberry

Cathy Nicholson

Claire O'Leary

Rosie O'Connor

Kyungeun Oh

Richard Orr

Joelle Owusu-Sekyere

Johnnie Pakington

John Parsons

Katherine Pawson

Esme Pears

James Peck

Giulia Perin

Sarah Phelps

Alex Phillips

Hyde Phillips

Charlotte Plester

Oscar Plewes

Barry PM

Justin Pollard

Rosalind Pollitt

James Pout

Robert Prance

Nisha Prasad

Neil Racz

Ilana Rakhorst

Hugh and Juliet
  Ramsbotham

Amy Rankin

Dayna Ransley

Elisabeth Ransom

Jo Redman

Julia Reinicke

John Rice

Ed Richards

Jamie Richards

Anne Richardson

Rebecca Rodgers

Chris Rogers

Anna Ross

Ariel Rubin

Bella Ryba

Alexander & Darren
  Sanderson

Jack Sandle

Jami Saunders

Mark Serocold

Shiplake College

Airi Shiroma

Zoe Shuttleworth

Charlotte Simmonds

Clarissa Skb

Nicholas Smallwood

Neil Smith

Toby Smith

Crystal Song

Patricia Springbett

Louise Starkowsky Dancause

Laura Steer

Karen Stevens

Kelly Stevens

Mark & Millie Stone

Robert Talog Davies

Lucinda Talog Hay

Robert Taylor

TDVB, JJVH, MHVK

Reiner Tegtmeyer

Sheena Thavenot

Scott Thomson

Anna Torres

Lauren Troake

Andrew Trotman

Alice Troughton

James Turnbull

John Turner

Martin Turner

Sophia Ufton

Lelia Valois

Katherine Verdon-Roe

Peter Viner-Brown

Hollie Vines

Fliss Vnukova

Mona von Petersdorff

Sarah von Petersdorff

Tamara von Petersdorff

Elizabeth Wan

Peter E. Ward

Anna Warner

Ed Warner

Louisa Waters
Patrick Watson
Gillian Waugh
Georgie Weedon
Karen Westropp
Amanda Whitby
Ben Willbond
Natalie & Rob Williams
Paola Wingrove

Nick Winnett
Anna Witt
Gwen Wonhof
Didi Wood
Isabelle & Henry Wood
Caroline Wynne Willson
Celia Wynne Willson
Guzel Ziyatdinova
Jason Zuzga

—